The Pavement
Bookworm

The Pavement Bookworm

A True Story

Philani Dladla

BLACKBIRD
BOOKS

First published by BlackBird Books, an imprint
of Jacana Media (Pty) Ltd, in 2015
Second impression 2016

10 Orange Street
Sunnyside
Auckland Park 2092
South Africa
+2711 628 3200
www.jacana.co.za

ISBN 978-1-928337-00-3

Cover design by Shawn Paikin
Set in Sabon 11/16pt
Printed and bound by Mega Digital (Pty) Ltd, Cape Town
Job no. 002676

Also available as an e-book:
d-PDF 978-1-928337-01-0
ePUB 978-1-928337-02-7
mobi file 978-1-928337-03-4

See a complete list of Jacana titles at www.jacana.co.za

Foreword
by Busani Ngcaweni

THE THING ABOUT WRITING A BOOK is that once it is published, you lose your innocence, your privacy and all the privileges afforded to ordinary members of society. Put differently, writing a book is like being elected into political office. Upon assuming this public position, you subject yourself to scrutiny, to praise, to a dipper measuring stick. You literately become a subject in the world of literature.

Through this book, Philani Dladla loses his innocence. Not that it matters much to him anyway, I suspect. After all, this chronicle tells tales of multiple losses, triumphs and opportunities. It tells the South African story of finding identity, meaning and being. Through the Pavement Bookworm, we are reminded of the pitfalls of power and privilege and the degrading consequences of neglect, poverty and deprivation.

Sometimes the story sounds unbelievable, a fiction existing only in Philani Dladla's imagination. Yet, each page represents the experience of many young men and women in post-apartheid South Africa. Young people who have lived through the perils of broken families and dreams deferred. Young people living through social, economic and urban transitions that come with lives led in homelessness, sexual assault, drugs and alcohol abuse. All in the midst of achievement, progress and social mobility which has been the experience of the majority of young people who have made good of progressive youth development policies.

Looking away is a common refrain for many who come across homeless people. We look at them with an irate eye: 'What are they doing here?' 'Why is he not at school?' 'Where are his parents?' Through this book, we enter the world of homeless people and their daily encounters with the 'outside world'. We are taken through the backward and forward journey of young people who end up in less desirable circumstances.

Looking away was also my attitude until I encountered the Pavement Bookworm through Ayanda Allie-Payne of SABC's *Morning Live*. I took on the challenge of helping a young homeless man make his publishing dream a reality. I could not believe that after all the spectacular international coverage he had received, he still struggled to get a publisher. But as I have said, when homeless people are involved, we tend to look away. Worse still, he is black and without a benefactor trying to break into in an untransformed industry.

Working with Philani to edit this book was an emotional rollercoaster and an intellectual stretch. The young man is brave. Brave for what he has survived and for his readiness to bare all. Very few young men would consciously tell the world about being sexually abused. Even fewer can make so bold a conclusion that 'my father is not my role model'. In a way, Philani spoke of my own life experience and those of many others who had fathers who made zero impact in their spiritual and intellectual growth. But I digress. Perhaps not an impossibility given the propensity of this book to touch a nerve, to bring one into a reality check.

This book is not about homelessness. It is a book about books, about the liberating and healing effects of reading. It takes creativity and courage for a young man in the era of social media to abandon one hundred characters and short-hand in favour of a more painstaking hobby: reading and now, through this project, producing a compelling semi-autobiography.

At the Pavement Bookworm Foundation (PBF), a platform we have created to help Philani Dladla advance his book reading clubs, we are inspired to invest social capital towards advancing the course of literacy and education among disadvantaged children. Like Philani himself, those who navigate the following pages should discover their conscience and purpose and proceed to work towards building a society we want and deserve to live in.

At the PBF we are ready to partner with likeminded

individuals willing to donate books, computers and calculators for distribution to township schools, the inner city, rural areas and informal settlements. Let us clear our closets and donate old conference bags which poor children can use to carry books to school instead of plastic bags.

After many hours of argument, doubt, cut and paste, we finally present this book to the world, believing this story of post-apartheid South Africa will change the way young people think of their invincibility and vulnerability.

– Busani Ngcaweni, book editor and
editor of Liberation Diaries

In the beginning there
was a book

BOOKS ARE A VERY IMPORTANT part of my life. Books are my wealth and pay my bills. Books have a magic that keeps me going through hard times.

I started writing this book on Friday 5 August 2011 on a piece of paper, just like Abraham Lincoln, who only had a pen and a sheet of paper available to him at that time. But I was sitting on the pavement on Empire Road in Johannesburg where I sold second-hand books. I love reading but felt I could write just as well as the author of the book I was reading at the time. So I took out a pen and started writing about my life as though writing a letter to my unborn child, as honestly as I could.

I fell in love with books at the age of 12. My first book was a birthday gift, entitled *The Last White Parliament* by Frederick van Zyl Slabbert. It was a gift from the man that my mother worked for, Mr Joseph Castyline. He promised me that if I were able to read it and tell him what it was about, he would get me another one.

The book was about South African politics, but because I couldn't read or speak English properly at the time I didn't know that. I was just another 12-year-old African boy who went to a school in a rural community in KwaZulu-Natal. IsiZulu was our main language, and our teacher only spoke isiZulu, even during English classes; she explained everything in isiZulu. I mean we were learning English in our isiZulu language. But that did not stop me from achieving my goal.

I started spending more time alone with my new best friend, that book *The Last White Parliament*. I played less and read more. I did not just read to kill time, but tried hard to read with understanding; I wanted to impress my mother's boss. Back in those days you were considered to be very lucky if white people liked you. I was lucky because the white people that uMa worked for liked me, Mr and Mrs Smith and later Mr and Mrs Castyline. All my mother's bosses liked me and they played a very important role in my childhood. I'm not sure I would've made it if uMa had not worked for such angels. They never called us *kaffirs*, like many white people called black people in those days.

My past made me who I am today and I want to take the opportunity writing this book presents to tell you about my goals and dreams. But first you have to know where I come from so you can understand why I have the goals that I have and dream the dreams that I dream. So in the next few chapters I'm going to take you back to my roots, before I was the Pavement Bookworm, before I moved to the City of Gold, before I received that first book.

—•—

My name is Philani Emmanuel Dladla. I come from a small, peaceful town on the south coast of KwaZulu-Natal called Port Shepstone. It's a town of summer rains and consistently mild temperatures. I know some people think being rich means having lots of money. Today I've come to know a different kind of wealth. Those people think I'm crazy because I have no money or flashy material things. People might define wealth differently, but I am rich. For me wealth is being able to give without remembering and to be able to write my name on people's hearts every day. I know that if I died today my kids from the readers' club that I started in Joubert Park and those who have been helped through the Pavement Bookworm Foundation would remember me and would tell their grandkids about the stories I once read to them. For me that is wealth, a legacy that will last for generations.

I'm wealthy because when I go to bed at night I sleep. I can sleep peacefully because I have no guilt. I know I haven't stepped on anybody's toes to get what I want. I know how to be satisfied with the little I've got. I believe that people who care more about money than they care about people are empty inside. Nothing will ever be enough to fill that emptiness.

Some rich people say that broke people *pretend* money isn't everything. Of course, I like the things that money can do for me, but I believe in people and not in paper and coins, because these have no feelings. Of course, money helps me help my kids and puts smiles on their faces when I buy them books or stationery or whatever they need for school. That's what I like, that's what makes me happy – putting money to good use. To me, merely accumulating money is pointless.

As you will read in the pages of this book, I've done stupid things in my life with money. I did drugs, drank alcohol, had unprotected sex and gambled. I didn't just gamble with money; I also gambled with my life. When I look back at my past and everywhere I've been, I wonder how I have managed to survive. I did things I'm not proud of, but I don't want to hide any of them or try to cover them up or pretend they never happened. I'm no saint and I *was* a bad guy. I might still be young but my past is filled with dark memories. Experimenting with drugs was probably the worst decision I ever made.

I'm sharing this with you, dear reader, because I want you to learn something from my mistakes. If you're wise you don't have to make the same mistakes. I'm sure you won't do the stupid things I did unless you don't care about your life, or you're one of those guys who always says *it won't happen to me*. I won't deny it; I was once one of those *it-won't-happen-to-me* type of guys.

Today I have nothing to hide because yesterday is behind me now. If I hide the truth and try to be perfect and act like the past never happened I'd be a selfish fool, because somewhere out there someone else is going through what I went through. Take it from me, drugs are bad; they make you think you're the wisest man on earth while you're actually the biggest fool under the sun. I was once that big fool.

But I digress; let's go back to the beginning.

The saga of my African family

My CHILDHOOD WAS NO WALK in the park. I remember how much it made us both cry, like we were reliving the nightmare, when uMa told me about the many hardships she faced and the hell she went through just to keep me alive. When I think about it I still cry.

This is my story. A struggling single mother, Ms Dolly Dladla, who never gave up, raised me in abject poverty. A fighter raised me. A survivor raised me; maybe that's why I also survived. Before freedom there was no Child Support Grant; no 50/50 rights for men and women. Men did what they thought was right. They did what they wanted to. A woman had no right to question a man's authority and simply had to obey even if she was against the man's decision. My mother was one of those women who never questioned her man's decisions.

Although my parents were not married, my father had paid *lobola* for my mother and so he had all the customary rights to take her to his home in a village called Mhlwasimbe when she was pregnant, where I was born. This is where my mother and I suffered abuse at the hands of my father's mother and sisters – I can't bring myself to call them my grandmother and aunts.

We lived in the same compound as his family but my mother had her own hut. Although we were supposedly eating from the same pot we were always hungry because those whose fathers were supporting the family by sending groceries were treated better than me. As my father did not send money and was always absent, we were the ones who suffered abuse from his family members. They did not go hungry but they did not like my mother. I think they hoped that if I died my mother would leave as she was only staying so that I would know my father's family. They never shared anything with her, not even soap to wash nappies. She used to pick *xubgwewe* (watercress) by the riverside, crush it and use it to wash our clothes. If she asked for food, she was told to *go and ask Philani's father to give you food*. Some people still remind me that I was called *ngwadule* – which means 'a land where nothing can grow' – because even hair wouldn't grow on my head from malnutrition.

My father's family valued cows more than human beings.

They really hated my mother and me. My father had a girlfriend who already had two sons with him, and they were always telling him that he was stupid because he wasted his father's cows paying *lobola* for my mother and not for Bheki and Xolani's mother. Bheki and Xolani were born before me.

I still believe that their taunting and stupid village family politics turned my father into the abusive man that he became. My father left my mother and me alone in the hands of his abusive family. My mother never knew where he was. He gave her nothing; not a cent. He never let anybody know where he was going. I believe my father never cared about uMa and me.

For the first year of my life, uMa struggled in poverty in his family home trying to raise me, trying her best not to give up. My father's sisters and his mother treated her like a slave. My mother told me I cried day and night because I was hungry. When she tried to breastfeed me her breasts were dry because she was also hungry and couldn't make milk. Sometimes, if I was lucky, uMa would ask the guys who milked the cows for some milk to feed me. Those boys also called me *ngwadule*. Even a simple porridge with no milk or sugar would have been a luxury for me.

Because I was malnourished, I was always sick as a baby. My mother was always hungry because they never gave her food. She used to walk a very long distance without shoes from Mhlwasimbe to Assisi District Clinic with me on her back. People she met on her way to the clinic told her to go back home and light the candles and mourn because they thought I was already dead. But she never gave up. She used every cent she could get her hands on to feed me, trying to make me healthy.

I know the reason my mother was treated poorly was because my father didn't send any money home to support us. By contrast, my father's older brother had a wife with whom he had a daughter and son. He had paid *lobola* for her and also taken her to live at his home in Mhlwasimbe with the same family that was treating my mother like a slave. The difference was that she was from a rich family. Her father was one of the first men to own many taxis and cars and other businesses at Oshabeni, a town in uMkhanyakude District in KwaZulu-Natal. This woman was treated like a queen, and she had everything that my mother didn't and her kids had everything I could only dream of. There was nothing there for my mother but suffering; she had only one hope – that maybe my father would come back some day and take us away from his evil sisters and mother.

Because I was always sick as a small baby, uMa knew that I would die if things continued the way they were. She risked everything and escaped early one morning with me on her back. Like I mentioned before, uMa had nothing, not even a cent, but people still had the spirit of *ubuntu* and a local taxi owner, Mr Mzelemu, gave her a free ride from Assisi Clinic to uMthethweni.

uMa knew her way around that area, so she went to the home of the Smiths where my granny was working as a domestic servant. Seeing how bad things were the Smiths didn't chase us out. They gave us accommodation in one of the back rooms. They gave my mother food and bought me baby food and medication. They took care of my mother and me until my health improved. They also offered my mother a job to assist my grandmother. My mother would go on to work for the Smiths for four years.

When Mrs Smith was sick, Mr Smith took uMa for a healthcare training course, which helped her to put many meals on our table long after the Smiths had passed away. Mr and Mrs Smith saved my life. If they had not welcomed us with open arms, I would've died. Even during the apartheid days, there were white people with good hearts who took great risks and made huge sacrifices like Mr and Mrs Smith did for us. They loved and spoilt me like their last-born child. I occupied the space of their children who had left home.

They bought me toys, medication and food when so many other white people would've said *let the kaffir die*. They saved my life and they reminded uMa how to smile again. The Smiths gave uMa more than just a reason to smile. They made me healthy and gave her a job and a roof over her head. They gave her the title *Healthcare Worker*. She knocked on their door with nothing but a crying, sick baby with a big head on her back, but she left their house with a healthy and happy child, some money and a qualification.

After leaving the Smiths house, following the death of Mrs Smith, my mother was employed by Mr Joseph Castyline to look after his wife. She used the experience and the reference from the Smiths to secure her new job as a caregiver to Mr Castyline's wife. She worked for the Castylines for many years. Even after Mrs Castyline passed away, uMa continued to work there until Mr Castyline died. After Mrs Castyline passed away uMa's job was just to clean the house.

We made a lot of memories with that good old man. I

remember the smell of the good food he prepared every time I visited. He read me good books and he was good to uMa, so she always looked forward to going to work. Mr Castyline was super cool and super kind. I wished that my father were half as kind as Mr Castyline. I visited Mr Castyline many times before he passed away, but the visit that stands out from all other visits was when I turned 12 because that's when he gave me that first birthday gift, *The Last White Parliament*.

It was like my father was waiting until uMa was happy again before he came back into our lives. My mother insisted they build their own house while uMa and I lived in my granny's house. My mother's uncle was a special advisor to the chief; he helped her to secure a piece of land under her own name back in the days when it was rare for a woman to own land.

My mother worked for Joseph Castyline for seven years, all the while supporting my father who, after being absent for I don't even remember how long, came back. She took him back and it was a nightmare because he beat us and abused us. He only came back after he lost his job at the laundry in Port Shepstone where he used to work. She had two more sons with my father during the next few years, my brothers Sabelo and Sphesihle. My mother had to put food on the table for my two brothers and my father and me.

Needless to say, we were very surprised when Mr Castyline left everything that he had to my mother when he died. Suddenly, here was a domestic worker owning all the belongings of her late employer. I still have Mr Castyline's will. She had a car, furniture, appliances and money in the bank. That man finished what he started. Since he was the one who got me addicted to reading in the first place, he left me more good books to read and own, just like he had promised.

All of a sudden, my father started respecting us. He was now behaving like a good child; my mother's 'overgrown first born'. He would be bought underwear, clothes and food.

As far as we know, this wise and bold lady, Ms Dolly Dladla, invested most of that inheritance by rebuilding her 2-room mud house for her four sons: that's my father, the late Khayelihle Lushaba, Sabelo Dladla, Sphesihle Dladla and Philani Dladla.

The first house uMa built was a two-roomed mud house. (I'm excluding my father as he did nothing to help.) Aunt Cynthia and her young brother, Malume Siya, helped build the house from start to finish. We now had a decent house at Oshabeni village. I'm still proud to call it home, the nice house my mother built.

I don't know any other domestic worker who built a house like the house uMa built for us. She didn't stop there. She also bought land next to our home and built a house for her mother Syleen and father John, her sister Cynthia and uncle Siyabonga. My older uncle, Sthembiso, was doing ten years' jail time. He didn't get to see his younger sister do the things that many brothers ought to have done for their parents. In my mother's day she was always kind to everybody, and shared as much as she could with our neighbours. Her motto was *giving is a gift to the giver*, and she did just that, giving and giving without remembering. In my community she made history, like her son is making history today. This will be the first book to be published that was written by somebody from Oshabeni. Since my mother has always been both a mother and a father to me I guess I'm qualified to say *like mother like son*. Don't get me wrong – I feel that I never had a father. My mother gave me everything that my father failed to give.

There are many housewives where we come from. But uMa never wanted to be one. She chose to work hard outside the home despite everything Mr Castyline had left for her. As fate would have it, she found herself with a househusband, her 'overgrown first-born son'. Mind you, this is the same guy who had abused us all for many years.

In the past women were not as confused as women are today, as they knew exactly what they wanted from a man. They wanted love. If true love never existed, uMa wouldn't have held onto an abusive monster like my father. She must have loved him, and love is blind. She still believed that he would change some day. Well, love only blinds the one who loves, not the bystanders. Our neighbours knew that he was not going to change. They knew what kind of man my father was. They knew that he was beating and abusing us. They heard us crying day and night. They saw what was happening but they were afraid of him.

In retrospect, one of two things was happening here. Either my mother was a faithful partner who wouldn't allow her new material status to change her or she was just naïve.

As for my part, I agonised, thinking, what other woman would tolerate this? Would they pack their bags and go or send the man packing? My father felt comfortable and decided that he didn't have to go job hunting. He decided to hunt animals in the jungle around the Umzimkhulu River instead, but that was no real job; it was just a hobby he did to kill time and take his mind off things. It didn't put food on our table or benefit us in anyway.

Besides, he was not a good hunter. You can imagine how hungry spending the whole day in a jungle can make a man, and extreme hunger makes a man angry, so you know it was an angry man who came home in the evening. My father had six dogs. He spent more time with them. He loved them more than he loved my mother and my brothers and me. My mother had a big yard at home and other kids liked playing marbles in my mother's yard but they all knew that when they saw my father coming they had to run for their lives – he used to beat anyone he found in uMa's yard, because he said it was keeping us away from our daily duty of cooking *pap* and bones for his dogs.

At home we were not allowed to go and play without cooking for the dogs first. If my dad found you playing on the streets without feeding the dogs you got a hiding. But my books helped me stay inside. I wanted to read and understand. I enjoyed it and it also kept me away from getting beaten because time spent with friends was accompanied by a hiding.

After a while, my father got bored of hunting so he decided to start a soccer team. That also didn't work, but my loyal mother was behind him all the way until he woke up from his dream and realised that it was just a waste of time.

My mother was always strong, always a fighter. She was a mother to her man and her children; yes, all of us were her children. If I could, I would raise my father from his grave so that he could testify that the lovely Dolly Dladla was his mother too, feeding his children and even his precious dogs, and on top of that buying him clothes, toiletries, even underpants! Love is blind because even after all the abuse we had suffered, uMa still loved him.

Nervous conditions

AT SCHOOL I was just an average learner, not very bright. I was passing my grades but I was not the smartest kid. Now that I spend most of my days surrounded by many kids, I clearly understand the reason why I never did well at school. No matter what your colour or race is, kids with abusive parents and from abusive backgrounds do not succeed in doing well at school (although, there are a few exceptions). My English was improving though, because uMa and I always communicated in English so that I could learn it quicker. Later on when my reading ability improved I used the dictionary most of the time to define and learn how to pronounce difficult words. Eventually this increased my vocabulary. Throughout all this, unknown to anyone else, I was struggling with suicidal thoughts.

Imagine wanting to die at the age of 16 just to prove I had rights and that nobody could tell me what to do? Perhaps if my father had spent more time teaching me about manhood than he spent with his dogs I would've made different choices in my teen years. Don't get it twisted; I don't blame him or anyone else for my stupid decisions, because I was free to make my own choices and nobody forced me. I won't lie and say that my father told me this or that, because as you know, he wasn't really there. He never even gave me his name. I will be Philani Dladla until the day I die. Dladla is my mother's surname and will always be my surname because they were not legally married. Like I said before, he only paid *lobola*. He didn't raise me; a struggling single lady raised me.

It was a tsunami at home after my father died. He died on 12 January 2000. We woke up in the morning to find he had died in his sleep. My father's family tried to kill my mother, two brothers and me. They accused my mother of being a witch and said she used *muthi* to kill my father. They sent men to kill us all, but the men they hired didn't have enough balls to perform the task that they were hired to do. They confessed to uMa, and warned her to be careful because his family had said they wouldn't rest until we were all dead.

They were angry that my mother made it against all odds. They didn't like it that the girl they used to abuse and call names had enough good fortune and financial power to build a better house than the hut that they lived in. They were calling me a dog and saying that uMa should just leave me to die because I was a waste of fresh air. When I look at them today I just feel sorry for them. Forgive me; I don't want to say that they are the ones who are a waste of fresh air.

I borrow the title for this chapter from Tsitsi Dangarembga's novel, *Nervous Conditions*, not because of my callowness but as an expression, like Dangarembga's main character, of my deepest feeling of what my father's death represented. It represented the end of patriarchal oppression. It represented freedom from abuse.

Why cry? After all, my father spent most of his time away from us. His death didn't change things, except now there was no one to beat us up and call us dogs. In my eyes we had always only ever had a mother. Only my mother missed my father. I don't know how she did it but uMa made us happy, she always had a plan. We had computers before most kids in my community knew how to use them. We had the latest cell phones that not even our class teachers had.

But I guess that was not enough for me. I felt like something was missing. After all the things uMa had done for me, I still had a desire to be cool. I wanted to be a part of the crew that was the coolest crew at my school. I did all that I had to do to impress them. I started smoking, fighting at school, making fun of other kids and not respecting my teachers. After some time, my dream became a reality and I became a crewmember. Our crew was a gang made up of stupid young troublemakers who did everything they could just to impress girls and be seen as cool. Selby Mkhungo, our crew leader, always reminded us how much girls liked bad guys. Being a crewmember meant a lot to all of us. We were the envy of many of our schoolmates and we were like a family, so if someone had a fight with one of us, he had to fight all five of us. I did a lot of stupid things to be seen as a cool guy. We saved our pocket money for beers on the weekend; we started drinking before the age of eighteen. After becoming a crewmember I went from being bullied to being a bully.

Eventually, I belonged. Finally I was validated. The love I received extended beyond the love I received from my mother.

But friends they come and friends they go, I learned that early in life. My best friend in my teen years was a guy called Doda Mbuso Ndovela. We grew up together. I had some of the best times of my life with that guy. One day my girlfriend came to visit but she brought her friend with her, so I had to call Doda and hook him up so that her friend could also have a date. The first time we spent a night with our girlfriends was in my bedroom. My mother's house had enough bedrooms for all of us – I had my own bedroom when most kids in my hood still used their parent's lounges as bedrooms.

Hey, but uMa was not at all happy with that. She woke us up in the middle of the night, shouting and saying; 'Hey Philani, what is happening here? Are you trying to turn my house into a brothel? Why doesn't your friend take his girlfriend home too? Is it because he's afraid of his parents and you are not afraid of me? Am I an easy target? Is it because I don't have a man in the house?'

I tried to tell uMa that my friend didn't have a bedroom at his house and that we didn't do anything with the girls, we were just sleeping and waiting for the sun to rise. But I lied – we did have sexual intercourse. I'm not sure about the girls, but for my friend and me it was our first sexual encounter. At first I thought my mother was a bad person for embarrassing me in front of my friends like she did, but when I think about it now she was right, I was disrespectful to her. She was just trying to teach me what is right. But when you're young and wild you do stupid things to impress your friends and girls. Young people do all sorts of stupid things just to be cool and thinking twice is the last thing on our minds. Regrets always come later and even though it happened a long time ago when I think about it today it's still embarrassing.

Some time after that, in 2005, I ended up being expelled from high school, when I was in Grade 12, because I was always causing trouble. I wanted attention, even at my own expense. I just wanted to be known as the coolest, most wicked guy around. That caused me a lot of trouble in the end. But my lovely patient mother never gave up on me. Sure, she knew I was a troublemaker but she gave me another chance. After all the hard times I caused her, she still cared a lot.

She told me, 'My son, I don't know who you think you're impressing with all these bad things you're doing out there, but you must remember one thing – you don't know how many days I have got left to look after you. You're not going to school for me or your friends but for yourself and your wife and kids.'

My mother managed to save enough money for me to study

towards an N3 Business Management course at a FET college (which is the equivalent of a Matric Grade 12) the following year, 2006. Looking back, I didn't learn anything from my stupid high school mistakes, because a few months after starting my studies, I started partying again. I wanted to be just as cool and popular as I was in high school and impress the girls and friends. Again it didn't end well – in fact this time things got more out of control. On 25 August 2007, I got stabbed while I was drunk and high. I can't remember what really happened, only waking up in hospital with a drip hanging over my head. I tried getting out of bed but I was too weak. It was hard to move any part of my body – I got badly beaten up before being stabbed, I guess. That was the most painful experience of my life. Being cool didn't feel so cool anymore.

While my peers were writing examinations, I was being nursed in a hospital bed. My mother and brothers and some neighbours were the only people who came to see me in hospital. Some only came to tell me what a bad boy I was and how much of a disappointment I was to my mother; others came only to see how bad it was and to say 'I told you so'. Not one of the girls that I was trying to impress came to visit me. Not even Mahlengi Gumbi, my girlfriend at the time, who seemed to be 'crazy-in-love' with me, came to see how I was doing. I was out of sight, out of mind.

More pain and hurt was waiting for me at home. After being discharged from hospital I remember how everybody used to look at me. Elders in my community warned their sons and daughters not to go near me because I was a bad influence. My girlfriend at that time broke up with me saying I was a serial loser and a joke. Those were the worst days of my life, because my friends turned against me, telling me how stupid I was for wasting my mother's hard-earned cash on girls, drugs and alcohol.

People in rural communities like gossiping. It got so bad that I ended up trying to take my own life by hanging myself. That suicide attempt didn't work thanks to my brother, Sabelo, who managed to save me before it was too late. I tried taking my own life more than once. Trying to hang myself was the most painful, but I also tried to overdose on tablets, which also didn't work. There's still a track on my neck that the rope left all those years ago. It's a painful reminder of what I was going through those days; I've tried removing it using different skincare products with not much success.

Today my childhood friend, Doda Mbuso Ndovela, doesn't care how much trouble I got into to just look cool in his eyes. When I got kicked out of high school, dropped out of college and tried to commit suicide he was one of the people laughing at me and calling me names. When his older brother started making money and became a taxi boss, he used every opportunity he could get to make me feel like a nothing, flashing money in my face, racing up and down the street in his mother's car with his new friends. Every time he saw me he reminded me of the days when my mother had a lot of money and when his family had not had much. I remember it like yesterday.

Should I stay or should I go? My life on the streets

MY MOTHER DIDN'T LIKE IT THAT PEOPLE were saying bad things about me and worried that it would push me closer to an early grave. In July of 2008 she decided that it would be better if I moved to Johannesburg. So I moved in with my mother's friend in Doornfontein. It felt good to be away from all the negativity and the judgemental people who had nothing better to do than to gossip and spread rumours. One thing I like about Johannesburg is that nobody sticks his or her nose in your business, although that can become a problem, because even when people see you being robbed or being beaten up they continue minding their own business.

My first job in Johannesburg was as a waiter in a restaurant called Gramadoelas at the Market Theatre in Newtown. Gramadoelas was one of the most famous restaurants in South Africa. Famous people used to walk in and out of it every day. People like Nelson Mandela, Queen Elizabeth, Denzel Washington, and many famous people have dined there. My boss, Edwan Naude, and his partner, Brian Shalkoff, were very nice to everybody who worked for them. I should have stayed there and served famous people every day like we did. But I wanted to save rather than serve people, so I did a healthcare course. From there I moved to being a healthcare worker at Johannesburg Association for the Aged.

At last things were going my way and life was getting better. I had saved thousands of rands that I was planning to spend on my education the following year. But, I thought, since we go to school so we can be employable and I already had a job, a permanent one for that matter, education could wait. So I used all the money I had saved to rent my own place and be more independent. I moved from the room I lived in to my own apartment. It was a much better and more secure place. The best thing about living in my own apartment was that I made my own rules and could decide to live by them or break them. Nobody told me what to do or when to do it. Life was good, but I guess I got too comfortable. I never did finish my Grade 12.

I started doing drugs again after two months of living on my own. I just wanted to know how it felt. My curiosity got the best of me. I had always wondered about the people I saw high.

I had heard about The Sense in Hillbrow, so I asked a homeless guy who used to ask me for money on the streets and he took me to The Sense. I told him I wanted to know what it felt like. He warned me that it would make me happy but that it could destroy my life. He told me that he had had a life, a good one, before the drugs. I just didn't think it could happen to me.

But this time I was not just smoking weed, I was taking stronger and more addictive drugs. I knew that it was wrong, but I said to myself, *Don't worry, you've got this.* My plan was just to have fun once and never do it again. I never thought it would get serious. I never thought that a once-only experiment would cause so many problems. I told myself I was just having a good time celebrating good times. I used to hear motivational speakers saying you should celebrate your victories. For me it was a victory that at age 21 I had my own apartment. Where I'm from, I see old men still living with their parents and feeling comfortable with it, men still asking their mothers what's for dinner every day.

I stopped caring about many things, including eating and taking care of myself. So paying rent was the last thing on my mind. Because I was still 'working' and had the right paperwork, I went and got a loan of R15 800 – all that I qualified for. I spent all that money on drugs. After that I started selling the few things I had one by one. There were days when I didn't pitch for work. I would wake up not feeling well from the cravings. And I just got lazy. I soon received my first warning. I didn't pitch again the very next day. After some days, I felt I couldn't face the shame of going after not pitching for so long. That is how I walked away from a good job; a job that I was good at. It is a shameful thing when you let down people who believe in you.

Within a very short space of time, I lost my job, my apartment, furniture, appliances, gadgets, my dignity and everything else that I worked hard for because of the drugs. I was no longer able to pay my monthly rental so I was kicked out of the apartment where I lived. I was only allowed to take a bag full of clothes, a blanket and a pile of books. I had nowhere to go. No friends, no money, nothing but problems, problems and more problems. I remember it like it was yesterday. I spent most of that day under a tree in Joubert Park with my problems coming at me. All I could think about was problems. For starters, I didn't know where to go from the park where I was sitting; where would I sleep? I owed more than R15 000 to a local bank for a loan. I should have used that money to pay my rent, but no, I used it to finance my drug addiction.

Under the influence of drugs, I was too stupid to remember that there's something called tomorrow. I had squandered everything I had worked for and was now homeless on the streets of Johannesburg. I couldn't call my mother and ask for help, or go to her friend's house because when I started doing drugs I changed my contact number and stopped calling her or sending money to her or my brothers.

It was a cold night in Johannesburg and it was getting late. I had to make a plan and look for a place to sleep. Trouble was, I didn't have friends or relatives living in Johannesburg. I was stuck all on my own. I remembered that I had seen people sleeping under the Nelson Mandela Bridge. I had no other choice; I had nothing to lose so I decided to go ask them for a space to sleep before it was too late. Homelessness is better in a group than to face it on your own. I didn't think it would be a big problem since I had my own blanket. I went there and asked them for a space to sleep, and they agreed to accommodate me, but there was a catch. They told me that we all know that there's nothing for free in Jozi. I had to give them my bag of clothes as a rental payment (they called it a protection fee). I didn't care about clothes anymore. All that mattered was that I would have a place to sleep that night and I could keep my expensive pile of collectable first-edition books that Joseph Castyline had left for me.

Johannesburg was very cold that night and my first night homeless was the hardest. The concrete was not as comfortable as my bed was. I didn't even have boxes or plastic bags to sleep on – only concrete. But that would turn out to be the least of my worries. It stank there from the smell of shit and urine combined with the body odour of the guys who occupied that space under the bridge. They stank like they'd never had a bath in their life and yet they were all comfortable with it. Some of the guys were busy interrogating me, asking all sorts of general and personal questions like they'd never heard the phrase *mind your own business*. Eventually they stopped questioning me.

Instead of asking me all of those questions, I wish they had bothered to tell me that while they were the bosses during the day, at night rats ran the show. The whole night rats owned the space. It was like they knew that I was new and they were trying to welcome me. I was afraid that they would bite me. I don't even remember what time I fell asleep because I was too worried about the rats.

I woke up to a chaotic morning under the bridge. No one

had time to waste. Everybody was busy getting ready to go hustle. The scene reminded me of the saying: *another day another dollar, boss.* I would find out that they all specialised in different professions, so they went off in different directions. Some specialised in selling pity, begging for anything from money, food scraps, clothes and blankets. Others specialised in recycling – they woke up early in the morning to go up and down the streets of Jozi looking for cans and paper to recycle. Recycling is not an easy job. The recyclers were known as magicians because they were able to turn trash into money.

My bookshop on
Empire Road

I SPENT MY FIRST MORNING observing my new surroundings, my new world. In the words of PW Botha 'adapt or die', I knew I would have to be a quick learner if I was going to survive there. The guys who were begging on the street corners were mostly *selling* pity and they were making good money from it. People were clearly buying it because they were giving them money. To this day I still struggle to understand why people were giving them money. Maybe it is because I lived on the streets and I know what that money was used for – drugs. The truth is, if you give a drug addict money, you're sponsoring his supplier. You may think you're being kind; but the money given to beggars is the reason why some parents are on their knees every night crying and praying that their sons and daughters come back home. That they keep receiving money, which they *will* use to buy drugs, is the reason some of them do not to go back home. When you give money to street kids you contribute to the many crimes and the lives that are lost because of the likes of *nyaope* and other drugs that these guys buy with all the money they get every day from begging.

Now that I am sober, I have come to know that if you want to help with your money, there are many kids who go to school with nothing to eat for the whole day, there are many shelters and orphanages and old-age homes that can really use your help. My life on the streets has exposed me to many tragedies. I have seen terrible things there and I don't want to see any more kids falling into a drug trap and possibly ending up like I did. I'm 100 per cent against drug usage. I'm 100 per cent against people who give money to drug addicts. People can see that drugs turn our youth into uncontrollable monsters, yet they still give them money to buy more.

There is nothing like hunger and desperation to make you to think out of the box, and fast. I had nothing to eat and I had nothing to smoke. Out on the streets, no one cared whether I had food or drugs or whether I was safe or harmed; I just had to survive on my own. I knew I had no time to waste or hunger would kill me. I had to find my own way of making money. There are no rules and it doesn't matter how you make your money, but you have to make the money so that you can have the drugs. If you can manage that then you're the man and you can live like a street king. I also knew, though, that I did not want to sell pity in exchange for cash. I wanted to give people value in exchange for their money. And so I walked to where Empire Road meets Yale Road at the entrance to Wits University, armed with nothing but my pile of books. I had already observed that the guys I had met under the bridge had street corners that they 'owned', where they'd been begging for many years. Most of the busy street corners were occupied, but the one at Empire and Yale looked more peaceful.

I started by making jokes with motorists, most of whom were university students and staff, about how little they knew about philosophers like Plato and Socrates and authors like Emily Brontë, Charles Dickens, Jane Austen, William Shakespeare, and many other authors and famous philosophers. Most people I met at the university entrance were much more educated than me, but it was unbelievable how little they knew about authors, novels and philosophy. Some didn't even know who Socrates was. Although he never wrote anything himself, I learned a lot from his students' work. He lived in ancient Greece from 470–399 BC and, according to my understanding, was the most enigmatic figure in the entire history of philosophy. I started sharing what little knowledge I had with motorists, giving them book reviews and recommending books and authors, criticising and rating their books.

My idea worked from the first day. I had struck gold! Most of the money went to funding my drug addiction and not my tummy. I didn't like it but there was nothing much I could do about it. I was officially a street kid and my books were helping me to survive. It went on like that for days, weeks and months. Some days were better than others. I used to get high and laugh at nothing with fake friends who I met on the streets and under the bridge, and then spend my nights crying and praying to God to help me regain control of my life. I pretended not to care but deep inside my heart was crying out for help.

Take it from me. Some homeless people don't really care about life or people, but most pretend not to care. Let me give you a few points to help you identity the ones that really don't care and the ones that pretend not to care. Observe. When you are on the taxi or bus, you will see beggars who will never make eye contact with you. Those are the ones who pretend not to care, but they know deep inside their hearts that they care; they feel embarrassed about themselves but just don't want to let it show. The reason why they don't make eye contact with people on public transport is that they know that there is a possibility that somebody who knows them might be on board. Same thing applies to those guys who recycle trash. Most of them wear those hats and masks that cover their faces because they don't want to be seen. See, even the homeless sometimes have pride.

When I started doing drugs, I stopped caring about the many things that I had cared about, including my own family. Drugs made me feel so good and became my best friend, and when I was high I could forget about the things I had lost. Family, girls, my job and even food didn't matter anymore. All I cared about was hustling for some money and getting high. They were in the driver's seat of my life, they controlled my thoughts and determined my every move. I felt like a stranger inside my own body. Without them I felt empty, and I depended on them to keep me going.

I knew drugs were slowly destroying my life but I just didn't care anymore. I had already lost my job, my flat, my furniture and everything that I had ever worked for. Besides, some of the guys I lived with under the bridge had lost much more than I had. Some were from rich families, some of them were highly educated and some had blown every last cent of what they inherited from their parents' estates on drugs.

When you're lost, just as I was, you use other people's mistakes to make yourself feel better. When I compared my mistakes to theirs – the rich and the educated – I felt smarter than them, but when I compared my mistakes to others, I felt like the worst idiot alive.

When I was alone I cried and asked myself, *Is this the end of me?* Is this how I wanted my life to end – as a useless junkie who only cared about getting high and laughing at nothing? A few months later my good friend, drugs, was not so good to me anymore. They had stopped making me feel good and started making me sick.

Once you get in,
you can't get out

While living under the bridge, I had a friend called Sihle. He had left home in the Eastern Cape to go to the University of Johannesburg. His parents thought he was busy with his studies and were sending him money every month. He could've been a success story but he was smoking his future away and living under the bridge with us, unbeknown to his parents. He chose to be a sad story like the rest of us. That's how dangerous drugs are. Others were not just smoking but also injecting themselves with drugs. Sometimes six people shared one contaminated needle and syringe. No wonder some of my friends died of AIDS-related diseases because one infected many. We knew it was only a matter of who would die first. We even made jokes about it and although we didn't care about life most of us were afraid of dying.

I always thought I would be the first to die. The drugs were killing me inside and the results were visible on the outside. My clothes were dirty and I stank. I avoided mirrors because I didn't want to see the damage drugs had done to me. I could go on for days without eating and my breath would stink like shit. But I couldn't go a day without drugs.

I would walk up and down Empire Road, sometimes under the hot South African sun for hours, giving book reviews and selling books to Wits University students, staff and visitors to get money for drugs. I told them about the authors I had read, and how good or bad their writing was. I told them about new book releases if I read about these in a newspaper or a magazine. I know it might sound funny, but yes, street kids have access to magazines and newspapers. People were paying for the information I shared. I was not making a fortune but they paid enough for me to get high and forget about my problems.

Despite my drug addiction I was getting paid for doing something I really enjoyed doing. And I learned a lot from doing that work. I got introduced to new authors and I learned more about books, like how many copies a book has to sell to be a best seller. I learned about which publishers sold the most copies and whose books have been translated into the most languages. But I was a drug slave, just another fool who worked for hours to make money so that I could blow it all in less than an hour.

Do not think for a second that I liked the life I was living.

Drugs were abusing me. I was not blind and could see what was happening to me but there was nothing much I could do about it; I felt powerless. Trying to go a day without drugs was like a suicide attempt – it made me so sick that not even a doctor could do anything about it. Life without crack, rock, *nyaope* and heroin was hell.

One day I saw a young man about my age, nicely dressed in some designer clothes, walking with his girlfriend. I felt anger welling up inside me. He didn't even have to say anything to me for me to not like him. I was jealous. My heart was filled with envy and unwarranted hatred as I looked at that young man in his nice fresh clothes. I looked at myself in my dirty stinking clothes and wished I was him; I wanted to hurt him, I felt like punishing him just to make him feel my pain.

'Look at that stupid cheese boy with his skinny girlfriend. Why don't we go make them suffer?' I told my friend.

He said to me, 'Brother, the doors at Sun City are always open, prison never gets full, it's easy to get in there but it's very hard to get out.'

I knew my life was the way it was because of the choices that I had made. The thing about choices is they have consequences. You are free to make a choice but after you have chosen, the choice controls you. This was the future I chose, to quote the title of Busani Ngcaweni's book *The Future We Chose*. Don't make the same stupid mistakes I made. Most of the friends I lost to drugs were bright and talented but they died too young because of the choices they made. Looking back at those years now, I still don't understand how I managed to survived.

Life on the streets

So far I have only given you a compact version of my life at Empire Road. Some of the memories from that time are hard to allow out and they still fill me with a lot of sadness. But I want to leave no stone unturned and so I will try to tell you everything. I will try to go into all the dark corners I have been into and all the fights I lost and won. The times when I was the victim and when I was the one causing others to suffer. Empire Road is where it all went down: murder, drugs, charity, smash and grab, assault, just about any criminal activity you can think of. Empire is not just a road, it's a hood. From the day I started selling books at Empire my life changed and from that day onwards I started seeing things differently. I have seen things that I thought only happened in the movies. No, it wasn't easy – I didn't even know the place very well. I was just following the guys who I lived with under the bridge.

The first good friend I made was Siyabonga. When I first met him, he was busy collecting paper and plastic, cleaning the street and begging motorists for some change and food. He asked me what my story was. I told him where I was from, where I lived and what drugs had done to me. He was not with the guys I lived under the bridge with, although they knew and respected each other. Siyabonga was more friendly, open and helpful than the others. I told Siyabonga that my idea was to start a mobile bookshop there on the streets, but he just laughed at me saying, *My brother, these people are heartless; they won't buy from you.* He said that the motorists only cared about rich people like themselves and they think they are in heaven when they are inside their fucking cars.

I asked Siyabonga how he had ended up begging for food scraps and coins at Empire Road.

He said: 'Hey, it's a long story my brother. I'll just give you the highlights because I have got to hustle now, brother. I was only 16 when I left home. Everybody was tired of me and my dirty work. I was just having fun but my drug addiction problem got worse every day. I started stealing money from home but before I knew it everybody became more careful with their money, so I started selling my belongings. Soon I ran out of things to sell, but I still needed drugs to keep me high so I started making friends with some notorious neighbourhood thugs. We were breaking in and stealing in our own hood and *emajaradini ez'ngamla* [white people's houses]. Some of my crew members got arrested but I continued stealing and breaking into people's houses, using all the tricks and knowledge they passed down to me. I was now working alone and got arrested a few times. Then I left home because I was running away from the enemies I made while I was still working with my friends.

'Now I'm only 22 but I have already caused so many people pain and stress and scars, I might even have killed a man but maybe he survived.'

Suddenly Siyabonga didn't want to tell me anymore. He said he had wasted enough time already and that he was there to hustle and not for the Truth and Reconciliation Commission (TRC). He said *Let me go try my luck on that flashy Mercedes S500*. While I unpacked my books from the bag I watched carefully as he approached the man in the Mercedes who didn't look very friendly. He opened his window.

Siyabonga greeted him with a smile, 'Hi sir, please help me out with some small change or food.'

The man listened attentively as Siyabonga begged. Then he just laughed out loud and said: 'My boy, go tell your brother Julius Malema to give you some food and money. Your brother Julius has got a lot of money. He is the one who should share with you, not me; I'm not your brother. Didn't you hear your brother Julius telling your people to kill my people?'

That man's words killed Siyabonga's spirit. He didn't have the energy to hustle anymore after that encounter. He came back to where I was standing to talk to me again. I told him not to feel bad about what that man said to him.

He said, 'Don't worry my brother, I have been on the streets long enough not to worry about people like him. He is just a dog like his slave-trading ancestors.

'Every day I beg people for food to eat and money to get high. Some people even bring me clothes to wear, but what they don't know is that I don't care about looking good or feeling warm, I only want to get high, so I sell the clothes and groceries I get and buy drugs with the money. I'm a combination of good and evil. I steal from people who have plenty and sell to people who don't have much. Some people see me as a bad guy and some see me as a good guy. I used to smash and grab but now I only beg and help people who are stuck. Maybe the car broke down or they ran out of gas or if they've got a flat tyre I help change it or get water if their car is overheating, I don't have much power but I do give a push if the car needs a kick-start. I also give directions to people who are lost. Because I'm from the streets, I'm like a navigator and I know all the directions to every little town in this big bad city just like a streetwise taxi driver. As I'm talking to you, my friends and I, *abo s'gidla waar* [the homeless], are helping the police stop the bad guys who smash car windows during rush hour traffic and grab handbags, laptops or whatever they can get their hands on from inside the car.'

I was still new to being homeless so I didn't know what a *s'gidla waar* was. I asked Siyabonga but he just laughed at me and said, 'Boy you live on the streets yet you don't know what a *s'gidla waar* is?'

He said my homework was to find out. 'My brother, these streets can consume you. This is a concrete jungle where the bad meets the evil so you better keep your eyes wide open and watch your own back here.'

Then he went back to his hustle. I continued arranging my books, ready to try my luck like he was trying his. After a few minutes a lady in her mid-30s jumped out of a white van with a stack of newspapers in her arms. Siyabonga crossed over the road to help her carry them. They looked heavy but he didn't mind. I saw how happy he was to be helpful to others. He called me over and introduced me to the lady saying *Dimamzo* (lady), *this is Philani*. He told me that she had been selling newspapers at Empire Road for many years and that I should always remember to show her some respect. She didn't look happy to see me there – maybe she saw me as competition because I was selling books. After the introduction, Siyabonga went back to his hustle and I went back to my books.

At first I didn't want to actually sell my books. After all, we had a long history together and they were my friends. These books were my inheritance from Mr Castyline. When I moved to Johannesburg I was already in love with books and took about 12 books with me. Some of them were first editions. My plan was to sell only the stories contained in the books, not the books themselves. I still wanted to keep the books – I suppose like having your cake and eating it. I never wanted to part with them.

I'm sure my idea sounded crazy; that's why when I told Siyabonga that I was there just to sell the stories in the books he thought I was just another crazed drug addict.

My plan was to sell book reviews to Wits University's people. I walked up and down the street with my priceless pile of books telling people to pick any book they wanted me to tell them about. Some thought they were smart. They picked books they'd read again and again like *A Tale of Two Cities*, *Wuthering Heights* or *Pride and Prejudice*. But I surprised them; you see I was not taking chances. I know my books just like I know my own history. I gave them synopses as good as if they'd just read the whole book again. I was pleased to see that they were impressed. I never asked them for money but they gave me money from the goodness of their hearts. I was even getting suggestions and ideas from people who liked what I was doing.

From day one people loved my idea. I remember a man gave me a R100 note because he liked what I was doing. He suggested that I start selling academic books and said that many students would buy from me. A woman called Enid went crazy over my idea and told me to come the next morning because she would bring me more books to sell. Books never go out of style. Even e-books have failed to get hardcovers and paperbacks out of style. I mean, how can you get your favourite author to autograph an e-book? It's been almost four years now and people still like and support my business.

Lady Enid didn't just promise to bring me books like some of the others who made empty promises. (Maybe they'd had too much good food and wine that night when they saw me on the street because I never asked them for anything.) Enid told me to be early because she would bring me the books and she did, out of the goodness of her heart.

The book donation from Lady Enid gave me the break I needed because I was able to review my special books and sell the others. I made a lot of money that day and most of it went to feeding my drug addiction. But some of it went to good use and I bought some food, toiletries and washing powder. I bought new jeans and a shirt and more books to read and sell. That was how I spent that hard-earned cash and it made a difference. From that day I was a clean kid, although I lived under the bridge and was always wearing the same clothes. I was always clean and smelt good because my clothes were always washed.

Keeping clean was hard work as every morning I had to fetch water from the broken water meter with a 5-litre bucket. I used the same bucket as a washing basin to wash in and a 500 ml cold drink container for drinking water and for brushing my teeth. Some mornings were so cold that when I got to the meter the water would be frozen. It went on like that for many months.

I remember how when I was starting out, that some people looked at me like I was crazy, especially my own black brothers and sisters. Some made funny faces and silly jokes about me. I was called many names: an educated fool, just a hobo who was a waste of a good education, a street professor. Some American wannabes went to school in their friend's car and every time they saw me they were like, *Hey, what's popping Prof, what have you got for your students today?*

But most people I was selling to were nice to me and kept telling me to keep up the good work. They told me that it was the first time they'd seen somebody giving book reviews and selling books on a street corner. Whenever they said that I told them, *There's a first time for everything*, and they laughed. I felt good knowing that people were feeling my style. That was the main reason I never gave up.

—◆—

All was going well until one morning when I got to my spot at Empire and things were different. Siyabonga was not the only one begging there that morning, he had some company – there were two other guys sitting on the pavement sharing a joint.

They had black bin bags in their hands and I could see that they were getting ready to beg. Those guys didn't seem happy to see me there, but I continued minding my own business and took my books out of my bag and started selling like I did every day. I looked at Siyabonga. I could see that he was scared of them; he didn't seem to have much time to talk or even reply when I greeted him that morning. Instead he ignored me as though we had never met. While I was trying to sell my books, one of the guys smoking a joint on the pavement on the other side of the road crossed over to my side. He looked at me with eyes filled with hatred.

'You don't belong here! Who are you? Where have you come from and what are you doing here?' he asked.

'I am Philani from Port Shepstone and I'm here because I'm selling books,' I answered.

'Did you come all the way from Port Shepstone just to challenge me? There are many streets in Johannesburg. What made you think you could come sell your shit on my street?' he continued.

'I'm just trying to make money. I didn't know you owned the streets,' I replied.

He smacked me twice in my face and said, 'Well, now you know. I don't like you here. While I was on a good holiday in jail, a stupid new face is busy spending my money.'

Damn, he wanted to slap me again but I guess something told him that I had had enough already.

He said, 'Maybe you don't know who I am? My name is Bongani and these are my streets and around here whatever I say goes. Right now I don't want to see you here, stupid bookman, so you should go, before I change my mind and beat you like a slave.'

Siyabonga came to my rescue and explained to Bongani that I was just a friendly guy who was not looking for trouble and that I was just there to sell books and get high like everyone else. For a moment it looked like he understood, but I guess he changed his mind. He demanded that I go stand under the tree where the ABSA investments sign was and wait for him to make enough money to go get high and on his return I would have to pay him tax money. I didn't give him a hard time; I did just as I was told. Cowards live longer and I didn't want to fight that guy. I gave him some space and I walked to the service station near Imperial Toyota and bought a packet of snacks and went back to wait under the tree for him to finish begging.

Bad luck and trouble

WHILE ENJOYING MY SNACK and my good book, *All or Nothing* by Elizabeth Alder, I was interrupted by a man who called me over. He asked who I was and what I was waiting for. I told him that I was selling books on Empire Road, and I was standing under the tree because I was taking a break.

'You've got brains and you look like a nice guy. I'm going to buy all your books, just wait for me to come back,' he said and smiled.

For some reason I believed him, not because he was driving a nice car but because he was friendly.

I didn't have much choice but to wait, even if he wasn't coming back, because I had to wait for that bully Bongani to finish begging so I could go back and sell. But if he did come back, it would be a bonus because I wasn't going to have to struggle to sell my books since he said he would buy them all. That would be my first day of being sold out. I was so excited, but I continued reading, killing time and waiting patiently for the white Mercedes SLK 200 to come back.

While I was wondering how I would spend the money I saw the white Mercedes indicate and park near Imperial Toyota. It was him. He opened his window and called me. I went running to his car with my pile of books. My mind was already on the money even though I hadn't thought about how much I would charge him for all those books.

The bad news was he had left his wallet at his office, he said, but the good news was that if I agreed to go to his office with him, he would pay me for all my books and a little something extra for my taxi ride back home. So I got in the car and he drove us back to his office. He was very friendly and told me a lot about himself. He made me feel like we had known each other for years, like we were of the same class.

He told me his name was Mr Train.[1]

We arrived at his workplace (I won't name the company, to protect me from being sued). It was a nice office building, and he parked in a spot that had his name on it. He told me

---

1 Not his real name.

to follow him and not to talk to anybody. We took an elevator up to reception.

I asked, *What if security asks me for my details at reception?* He said they wouldn't because I was with the boss. Being the kind of guy that I am I did as I was told, and besides.

Nobody asked me anything at reception and I didn't say anything to anybody; I just followed him. We took a lift to his office on the top floor. It was the biggest office I'd ever seen in my life. It was bigger than the bedroom I had before I was homeless. He locked the door and asked me not to worry about anything. He told me that he only wanted to play with me and that if I played with him nicely he would pay me twice the amount he would've paid me for my books and I'd still get to keep my books.

When I asked him what game he wanted to play with me he said, 'Come on Philani, don't act like you don't know. Please show me your cock, don't be shy, and don't think too much about it. It's just you and me here, no one will see or judge us. I only want to play with it.'

He asked me if I needed something to drink. He had a mini-fridge loaded with all sorts of drinks, except alcoholic beverages. I told him, *Still water will do,* and he gave me a bottle of water and continued begging me to take off my pants.

I guess he was used to being begged by poor people like me and not being the one doing the begging because suddenly he got pissed off.

'Hey! I know you want money and you know what I want. If you don't want to play with me, you'll go play with the inmates in jail because I'll call security and tell them you're an intruder and a thief and that you were trying to rob me.'

'I'm going to tell Security the truth,' I said.

He just looked at me and laughed. 'Do you really think that they will believe you over me?'

He was no more Mr Nice Guy. He looked really pissed off. I knew that because he was a big shot, arranging my trip to jail would be like, hey presto. I hadn't made any book sales for the whole day, I was hungry and craving the drugs and I really, really didn't want to go to prison.

So I asked him how to play his game. He told me to relax and take off my pants, which I did. He grabbed my cock and played with it until it was hard. He was in a good mood again. His smile was back on his face, but I was still scared. He told me to put my pants on again. I was relieved that the nightmare was over.

He said, 'See, I told you that I won't bite, what were you afraid of? Come, follow me.'

He unlocked his office door, and I followed him to the lift. I was happy when he pressed the button for the ground floor because I thought we would go to the carpark. Little did I know, there was a gymnasium where he took me straight to the showers and instructed me to take off my clothes and take a shower. He brought me his shower bag that had everything he needed to make me clean and smell fresh.

That was one of the worst days of my life. The only good thing about all that madness was I had a chance to bathe with hot water after a very long time of washing in my 5-litre bucket with ice-cold tap water. He didn't let me enjoy the hot shower that day though. He was hurrying me up and telling me not to waste his time. I had a feeling that he was panicking and if

I tried fighting him, I might have won, but security was tight in that building. He used his access card to go everywhere and I didn't know how many security officers were on duty that afternoon. I realised that trying to be smart would end in a quick trip to Sun City Prison.

I think that the guy was very horny because, back at his office, he was not beating around the bush anymore like earlier. He took off his clothes and asked me to do the same. He kneeled in front of me and played with my cock until it hardened, then he sucked it. This was my first ever blowjob in my entire existence. I told you, dear reader, that I would tell you my life story as it happened, so judge me if you want to. It won't break me. I have seen, experienced and survived worse.

Don't get me wrong, I was against what he did – he raped me, but there was nothing I could do about it. As long as it didn't kill me I had to let him do whatever he wanted to with me. He could call Security and make up a story, and they would call the cops and tell them to lock me up and throw away the key. What would you do if you had a gun to your head?

Now my worst fear was that he would ask me to blow him too, but surprisingly, after all that playing, he still wanted more. It was like he was greedy and he couldn't get enough of my cock. He was kissing me and playing with my cock while the other hand was all over me. After awhile he took a lubricant out of his bag and applied it to my cock then on his rectum. He lay on the very thick and soft carpet and asked me to lie on top of him and penetrate him with my cock. We didn't even use protection, but I did as I was told. He was enjoying every minute of it. He was busy making sounds like a woman. With the kind of noise he made, I don't know if maybe his office was soundproofed or if he knew no one else was in the building. He praised me, telling me how good I was, telling me not to stop and how much he loved me. When his phone started ringing he ignored it and told me not to stop. I continued until we both climaxed. After we both calmed, he continued caressing me, telling me how nice it was, how much he enjoyed it and that he wanted us to do it again.

He asked me if I wanted to go home with him, but I was craving drugs. I refused his offer and said I wanted to go home. For a moment he didn't say a word but just stared at my private parts. I was afraid that maybe he was thinking of cutting it off and taking it home with him, since I had refused to go home with him. My craving for drugs became stronger, and I started feeling sick. I begged him to let me go now that I had given him what he wanted. He said, 'Okay, get dressed,' and gave me a towel to wipe my private parts. We both got dressed and while he was busy on his phone, he asked me if I needed anything to drink. The only thing I wanted was to get high. I said, 'Yes I'd like something to drink on my way home.' He asked me where home was but I didn't want to tell him that I lived under the bridge since he had already taken advantage of me and I didn't know what he would do next. I told him that I was from Port Shepstone, but I lived in downtown Joburg. He told me that he grew up in KwaZulu-Natal and that he owned a beach house at Uvongo.

We made our way out of the office to the parking lot. He opened the boot of his car and took out R600 from his wallet. Before he gave it to me he made me promise to keep it between us and not to tell a soul about what had happened in his office. I was surprised because he had told me earlier that he had left his wallet in the office. I became clear to me that he had been doing 'this' for some time and that he knew how to make people believe him. He asked me if that was enough and told me that he would've paid me twice that amount if I were willing to go home with him. Yes, I needed the money but that man seemed to have forgotten that he did all those sexual acts against my will and I was craving drugs and could no longer go on without them. I told him to drop me off at Constitution Hill. He didn't mind taking me there. Before we said goodbye he gave me his business card and told me to call if I needed anything. I was surprised to see from his card that he was the General Human Resource Manager of one of South Africa's biggest state-owned companies.

And yes, I used the R600 that guy paid me to buy drugs. Let me break it down for you – I had a few hundred rands that I didn't know what to do with except to smoke it. I went straight to our secret location in Hillbrow (The Sense) to get some good stuff. I bought ten bags of *nyaope* valued at R20 each, ten *rocks* valued at R20 each, ten fake cigarettes valued at 50c each, a pack of rolling papers for R4, a *skens* (dry weed leaves) and two match boxes for R1. I felt like I owned the world with all those drugs to myself.

The thing about drugs is they make you greedy. When you're new in the game you might have a smoking partner, but when you're addicted, you avoid others. If you do happen to sit together everyone smokes his or her own stuff – we call it the *every kid plays with his own toy* game. I went to my corner in the park where the other addicts chilled and made my joint and smoked. I melted a rock in my glass pipe and I smoked it and felt like I was in a new body. Then I crushed the weed and mixed it with some cigarette tobacco (*skens ne mix*), poured it onto a rolling paper and arranged it nicely before unwrapping the *nyaope* and carefully pouring it on my *skens ne mix*.

I rolled the joint nicely, making sure that I wet it with saliva to make it last for a long time and to prevent the wind from causing it to burn faster. After smoking that joint, I felt like I would live forever. I didn't care where I was or who was next to me, I felt like I was the only guy in the world. I felt sleepy but knew that if I closed my eyes I would be robbed blind and that I would wake up with not a cent or anything to smoke. *Rock* was the only solution. Rock is like an energiser – it gives you energy you didn't know you had. You can fight until you kill your opponent or die after smoking rock. You can dance until morning after smoking rock. Even when having sex, you can go until your partner begs you for mercy! It is one of the best performance enhancers. I took out my glass pipe and melted a precious rock and smoked it. After that I felt like I was Superman. I didn't feel sleepy any more. I had enough energy to walk from Hillbrow back to Braamfontein without feeling tired or thinking about what Mr Train had done to me.

I still had some change from the R600 but I didn't buy anything to eat when I made it back under the bridge. The guys were busy bragging about who made the most money and bought the most drugs that day. Sure, I had more drugs than most of them but I didn't want to join their stupid bragging game because then they would ask me for drugs or steal my money later that night. The only stupid mistake I made was to become a drug addict, but I still had brains in my head. I was smarter than that – I knew that their attention came at a price.

I was already sick from drug cravings and now I felt even sicker about what had happened with Mr Train. I had read in the *Encyclopaedia of Sexual Knowledge* that it is not easy to stop homosexual tendencies if you experience them in your adult life. I didn't want to think too much, I wanted to leave that experience in the past where it belonged. I didn't really want to go into the deeper details of what had happened; maybe I was scared to find out the truth. My main concern was to smoke enough until I healed from the encounter. So I rolled another joint, spiced it up with the mixture of heroin and whatever else they mix with it to make *nyaope*. Most of us didn't even know what was mixed together to make *nyaope*. We only knew that it made us feel good. To tell you the truth, I didn't even know how it was spelt till I started working on this book. I didn't want to heat a rock because it would keep me up all night, and the last thing I needed was to stay up all night thinking about what happened in that office that day. Luckily, I fell asleep shortly after that last joint.

The next morning, I still had drugs left over and some change, so I decided not to sell books on Empire Road that day. I knew that the crazy gay man in the white Mercedes would come looking for me. I knew that he was thinking about me. I spent the day under the bridge smoking drugs, reading my book, falling asleep, waking up and smoking again. I only went out to buy *amagwinya* (fat cakes) and some fruit. In the afternoon when the boys came back from the hustling game they asked me why I hadn't hustled that day. When I told them I was not feeling well, they laughed at me and said that I would smoke *not being well* then. They didn't know that I had something to smoke.

The next morning I went to fetch water from the broken meter so I could wash and go sell books on Empire Road. When I got there three hours later, Siyabonga came to tell me that he knew why I hadn't come to sell my books the previous day and it was because I had found myself a bitch. He said the white Mercedes SLK had come looking for me and that he knew the guy behind the wheel. He said there are many male prostitutes who sleep with men for money to buy drugs. They are isolated and are always being bullied and called names, and that he didn't want to see me being labelled as one of them because it would make my life extra hard.

The next day I sold only in the morning but then I realised that I couldn't hide from him forever. The following day I decided to go to his workplace to tell him that he had abused me and I would report the matter to the police if he ever came looking for me again. So I woke up early and made sure that I didn't look like I was living under the bridge. After bathing, I spent more than an hour making sure that I looked my best, combing my hair, brushing my teeth before and after my morning joint, then rushing down to Parktown to sell my books.

I talked to as many people as I could, trying to sell as many books as fast as I could, knowing that I didn't have the whole day because I had to confront him before he could come back again. What if the next time he were to ask a guy like Bongani, then I could lose my sleeping place or worse, the spot where I sold my books. Because he kept coming back asking for me, I would be labelled a sex trader and bullies like Bongani would be more than happy to get rid of me by burning my books or like what happened to this other guy called Jack who was stoned to death because he wouldn't surrender his drugs to drug addict bullies just like Bongani.

I had a friend who worked at Wits University – I don't know her name – but she drives the same red Porsche she drove back then because sometimes I see her driving past me in Greenside. She gave me a bag with some books in it to sell and made my life easier that day. The bag she gave me looked much nicer than the old bag I carried my books in. I wanted to look my best because I was going to go to that guy's workplace. I did not want to be called a hobo and get thrown out by the security guards. If a boss says, 'Security, come throw this man outside', it makes them very happy to oblige. Most security guards are black and black people derive joy from making blacks feel pain. They become powerful, in deed and imagination.

When I got to Mr Train's workplace, the receptionist called his personal assistant who told me that her boss was out of town but would be back soon. She gave me his contact number written on a piece of paper. I should have gone to the police station to open a case the first day, but I was afraid and embarrassed. I knew the police liked making fun of people with cases like me. I was embarrassed to even talk about it to my closest friend Siyabonga. Today I still find it hard to talk about and I feel dirty when I think about it, because in my Bible sodomy is a capital sin.

Eventually I did open a case against him, but the justice

system failed me. The company he worked for protected him. The investigating officer for my case told me the case was closed because the man had appeared in court but I never showed up. The investigating officer knew the spot where I sold books on Empire Road and had met me there more than twice but claimed he didn't know where to find me on the day I was due in court. The court decided to let him walk free on his first appearance without hearing my side of the story. The office where he worked has CCTV cameras in the building and I want to know why the videos were never used. That's what money can do for you in South Africa. You can get away with almost everything. The company he worked for cared only about protecting their name. I didn't have the kind of legal team that he had and I had failed to show up for my court date. This whole case was like one of Lee Child's *Jack Reacher* thrillers. The prosecutor told me to forget about the whole rape thing and move on with my life because it was just my word against his. What I need in my life is to forget about the whole experience and I suppose there is a form of justice at work because he was fired with immediate effect. Though he tried fighting it at the CCMA (Commission for Conciliation, Mediation and Arbitration), he didn't get re-instated.

A bend in the river and things start to change

BONGANI, THAT HEARTLESS BULLY, showed up at Empire Road while I was thinking about what had happened with Mr Train. I knew he would order me to stand under the tree until he finished begging. It was like I read his mind because that was the first thing he said when he opened his mouth. I didn't mind because I expected it. I packed my books and left him in peace for a while. I didn't like the idea of standing under the tree and waiting for his permission before I could continue selling so after a while I went back to Empire Road to see if the big boss was done begging. Fortunately he had gone – only Siya and Dimamzo were left. Dimamzo's newspapers were sold out and Siya was taking it easy that afternoon and was busy bragging about what a striker he was and how much money he had. I was the only one who hadn't made money that afternoon.

He advised me that we had to quit drugs and gave me some tips. I asked him that, if he knew an easy way out of drug addiction, why he wasn't taking it and becoming a free man again. The only easy and painless way out, he said, was to drink lots of alcohol so that you only wake up with a hangover and not that painful craving for drugs. He told me that it works for some people but not for others, although if you were a new addict chances were good that it could work for you. I liked his idea – after all the tears I cried every night and all my prayers, there was still hope and a way out. For me being an alcoholic is still being a drug addict, but an organised one, because alcohol is a legal drug, and if you drink responsibly you can still enjoy life and succeed.

When you're an addict of illegal drugs there's no such a thing as getting high responsibly – you get high, you want more – there's no limit. I'm not praising alcohol, but if you drink alcohol, you don't have to worry about the police, except if you're a drunken driver. With the kind of drugs I was using, you had to avoid a policeman and his sniffer dog, so for me being an alcoholic would be much better than being a drug addict.

Don't get it twisted. Just like cocaine, crack, weed, tik, heroin, or the master destroyer *nyaope*, I know that alcohol can seriously damage your mental health, your looks, or get you into serious financial trouble. Being drunk and risky sexual behaviour are best friends and can cause you to get infected with HIV or any other sexually transmitted diseases. For a girl it can lead to even more problems – a girl can get both sexually transmitted diseases and have an unplanned pregnancy, after just a few drinks. People who are drunk always insist that they are okay. When you're drunk you automatically become a target for criminals, which is why people get robbed, raped, attacked or hijacked mostly when they're drunk. Teens can agree to have sex with more than one guy, or even strangers, and get videotaped, all because they had one too many drinks. When the tapes go viral, it often leads to the suicide of those involved.

But I looked on the bright side. You know why I decided that alcohol was better than all those drugs I used? Alcohol can be enjoyable. Out there are many successful people like lawyers, doctors, entrepreneurs, politicians and celebrities who drink alcohol to celebrate certain special occasions. Those are the successful alcoholics. Some of them know their limit but some just don't know when to stop.

Something that I have realised is that a mistake some people make is to think that drug addicts and alcoholics are only underachievers. Just because they made some stupid mistake and started doping or drinking nonstop they are called good-for-nothings. I don't call them good-for-nothing, what I do is pray for them; honestly I believe that they can still change and make this world a better place. All they need is a push in the right direction. They need your help, good people!

God is God no matter what you call him in your language, and God doesn't make mistakes. When you see people who are lost, or need your help, and you call them all sorts of names like good-for-nothing or useless, do yourself a favour and look in the mirror and tell me what you see. All those people who you drive or walk past every day and think of them with so little regard are also images of God just like you are, and they make mistakes, just like you do.

How would you like to be called a good-for-nothing, useless thing because you made one silly mistake that changed your life forever? This is life, not a novel. You have read so far because you want to know more about things you never cared about before. You bought this good book, so be honest with yourself, and answer that question. You're here to learn more about things you see every day. We've seen highly successful people and super talented superstars lose their lives, fame and fortune because of drugs and alcohol. Some are still alive but doing time behind bars. Some are eating sardines when they used to eat sushi. Are they *all* good-for-nothing useless things, or did they simply make some stupid mistakes? Just like we all do sometimes.

But let me get back to that day.

I didn't make many sales for the rest of the day but I managed to sell two books to a lady who gave me R200 and told me to keep the change. For a drug addict who lived under the bridge, that was a lot of money to make in less than three hours. I had been listening to Siyabonga for most of the time and sold the books a few minutes after he left.

I packed my books and walked slowly up to Hillbrow. From that afternoon I decided to drink two beers every time I smoked to see if Siyabonga's idea would work for me. I bought enough stuff to cover me for the rest of the night and next morning. I went straight to my corner at the Smoker's Paradise (that's what we called the park where we used to smoke). Then I had two beers at a nearby tavern to kill time – I had nothing better to do, and a tavern was warmer than under the bridge. Beer didn't taste as good as it used to after not drinking for such a long time. I felt like I would vomit. I knew Siyabonga really wanted to help me. As I drank the beer that I wasn't even enjoying I hoped my friend's idea would really help me win over my drug addiction. I believed him. He had smoked drugs for many years before I ever thought of trying them. He always told me not to waste my life like he wasted his with drugs, especially *nyaope*. I knew he knew what he was talking about.

⎯⎯•⊪•⎯⎯

I wanted 'out' with the drugs, but alcohol was not the easy way out that I thought it was. Alcohol only made things worse. Alcohol led me to almost take own my life. The thing about drugs is that they made me happy because I could forget about my problems. That day I was about to discover that alcohol depressed me and made me think more deeply about my problems.

I hadn't made too many sales so I left my street corner early. The sun was hot and Siyabonga wasn't hustling on Empire so it was a boring day. I went to Hillbrow to score like I did every day. After getting high, I decided to buy beers with the change I had. My clothes were clean. I didn't smell like I was from the streets. The bag that I carried my books in was clean. Nobody could tell that I was homeless.

I was already high so I didn't need a lot to get drunk. After a few beers alcohol showed me flames. It was the boss and in comparison, I was just a small boy. I played some of my favourite songs on the jukebox. I played a song called 'Go on and Cry' by Bloodstone that caused me so much sadness and depression. I sang along as loud as I could and people looked at me like I was crazy. Maybe they thought a girl had dumped me because the song is about a failed relationship.

The more I drank, the more meaningless my life seemed to be. I decided that I would kill myself that afternoon. I was drunk but I was still afraid. I was not crying because I was drunk or crazy, I was crying because I was afraid to die. There were many voices in my head. One voice was telling me, 'No Philani, you're still too young to die. God created you for a reason', and another voice was telling me 'Yes Philani, God created you for a reason, and that reason is to suffer. Maybe if you die, you'll be at peace ... no more slaving around for Nigerian drug dealers.'

When you reach the end, you start thinking about the beginning. I thought back to all the dreams that I had and everything I wanted to be when I was a kid. When I looked at myself then I was none of these things and I wanted to die. I thought of throwing myself into the path of a speeding vehicle but that was just too scary. I still had some money so I bought some pain killers and laxatives to overdose on. I went upstairs to the tavern's toilets and opened a bottle of tablets and I poured them into my palm and swallowed them all. I opened another box of pain killers and swallowed those too. I looked myself in the mirror and tears were running down my face. I washed my face in the running tap water, cupped my hands under the tap and kept drinking water and swallowing the tablets until I had taken them all. After some time, somebody walked into the toilet and saw what was happening but it was already too late – I had swallowed all the pills and was already feeling dizzy and my stomach had started cramping. I don't remember what happened after that. I must have fallen and knocked my head on the wall and lost consciousness. I remember the pain I felt in my sternum. When I opened my eyes paramedics were all over the place. But I was confused, their lips were moving but I couldn't make sense of what they were saying. I could see, though, that they took my vital signs – pulse, respiration and blood pressure. I was then rushed to Johannesburg General Hospital.

When I arrived at the hospital I was still drunk and confused but I could answer their questions much better than when they took me from the pub. I can't remember the name of the nurse who interviewed me and filled out some documents, but she was sweet and beautiful. She asked me questions like my name, how old I am, where I'm from and if I knew where I was and where I lived. I didn't tell her that I was homeless because I was embarrassed. She asked me more and more questions and it felt like I was being interrogated by an attractive police officer. Later I was seen by the doctors. I was lucky because they didn't steal my bag of books at the pub and the porter helped wheel my bag and me to a ward on the fifth floor. Being hospitalised was no fun business, especially being woken very early in the morning, although it was a luxury for me to sleep indoors with warm blankets instead of under the bridge with only one blanket on cold concrete.

I complained but the nurses told me that I was in hospital not in a hotel. The nurses were rude and rough. In the morning I was sick with drug cravings, the stomach cramps were killing me and I was weak from vomiting after every meal. I needed drugs and thought that I would die. I ended up telling the doctor the truth, thinking that he would give me something to calm my cravings, but all he did was put me on a drip which he said would clean all the drugs from my system and ordered some medication that the nurses would give me after lunch.

The first few days in hospital were very hard, as I felt like everybody was against me. No, I felt like they hated me. It felt like I was in prison where the doctors were prison wardens and the nurses were prison guards. I tried escaping but I was too weak and the hospital security was able to stop me before I could make it to the main reception. I told the doctors that I needed drugs but they didn't care about that. They told me that I was in hospital and that their job was to save lives, not to destroy them. They told me that drugs are killers, as if I didn't know. When I started fighting and shouting and calling the nurses and doctors all sorts of names they put me in restraints and I was treated like a real prisoner in hospital. For two days I was cuffed until I calmed down.

As the drug cravings wore off I began to cooperate and things became easier. I realised that the nurses and doctors were not as bad and evil as I had thought and I started appreciating them. It was clear they were just trying to help me not harm me. I was moved to the psychiatry ward. I tried refusing, telling the doctor that I wasn't crazy. She said that she knew I wasn't crazy but because I'd been doing drugs for a long period of time, and because I have a mental condition called bipolar mood disorder, that I would feel better after treatment. She explained that bipolar disorder is a mental illness that affects how you feel, not how you think. That explanation didn't make any difference to me. All I could think about was that I had a mental illness that I knew nothing about. I know how people are when it comes to illnesses, especially mental illnesses. If you tell someone that you have a mental illness, they will think you're crazy, or stupid or call you all sorts of names, almost like the stigma attached to HIV/Aids. What was on my mind was the stigma. The same stigma applies to mental illnesses – people don't want to be seen around you because they don't want to be judged the same as you.

The psych ward looked more like a prison cell than a hospital ward, but luckily without the gangs in there and the nurses there friendlier. The ward was clean and smelt better than the one I had been transferred from. That ward had smelled like death. In the three days I was there I saw more dead people than most people see in a lifetime.

There was a lot of funny stuff happening in the psych ward. It was like we were locked into a room with clowns who didn't need to be paid to perform because in there guys were really crazy. Each day was different and some days the ward turned into a madhouse; patients ran around naked, some broke things, some fought, while others tried to have sex with the nurses running after them, trying to stop them. I learned and saw a lot from my days in that ward.

The problem with mental illness is that only your actions and behaviour can show the psychologists and nurses the degree of your illness, which is why doctors keep patients in psych wards and in mental institutions for such a long time. Doctors in the psych field have to guess most of the time; they work on what the patient tells them and often don't follow up to see if the statements made by the patient are true. The most important thing for them is to ensure their patients take their medication.

My hospital stay took a lot off my mind. I didn't have to worry about what to eat, I didn't have to worry if it was raining or snowing because I had a reliable and warm shelter over my head. I had enough time to read my books, and I went for weeks without street drugs. My problem was my roommate Lucky, who was schizophrenic and sometimes he acted really strange and that scared me.

I learnt that schizophrenia is a disorder that affects the way you think and the types of thoughts you have. The word *schizophrenia* literally means 'split mind', because there is a split between the person's mind and reality. Lucky would do all sorts of crazy things and interrupt me while I was trying to read. He had this crazy idea that he was God and would go around the ward praying for the patients and nurses and telling us that he was a black God.

He told me he could read minds and that he could fly, so you can imagine how hard it was sharing a room with him. I tried to treat him with respect because I had learned that most mental problems are caused by family history (genetics), life's problems like child abuse, brain chemicals, drug and alcohol abuse, and if a person is schizophrenic, it doesn't necessarily mean that they are bad or dangerous people. It is treatable and a person suffering from it can lead a successful, happy and productive life if their mental health is well looked after. But I'm sorry to say I lost my cool when I woke up one morning to find Lucky tearing up the book I was reading then. I was so angry I couldn't control myself and I started beating him up. He tried fighting back but I couldn't stop. The nurses tried to break up the fight but neither of us would give up so they had to call Security.

Lucky was badly injured and thus ended my comfortable stay in the psych ward at Joburg Gen. I had been there for less than a month. I was sorry for what I had done to Lucky over a book but you can't undo your actions. I felt bad as I'm not a violent guy. I think I lost my temper as I felt like I was part of the story and when Lucky destroyed the book I was prevented from knowing how it all ended.

I had made things worse for myself once again.

I was transferred from Johannesburg General Hospital to Sterkfontein Psychiatric Hospital. I was scared when we arrived because it looked like a prison and I thought I was being imprisoned for assaulting Lucky and for damaging the hospital's property. I was relieved when a doctor took my vital signs, opened a file for me and told the nurse to take me to Ward Number 8. From the outside, Ward 8 looked like an old abandoned building. We met a young-looking white man called Staff Nurse Mike, who took it from there. Staff Nurse Mike showed me around the ward and told me what to do and what not to do. He gave me a list of the ground rules. We were only allowed to smoke after meals. In Sterkfontein, you eat five times a day, so you can only smoke five times a day, one cigarette after every meal. He showed me where the public phone was. We were only allowed to make three phone calls a week and patients were not allowed to keep money. If I had visitors who gave me money, I had to register the money at the office and the nurses would give it to me when it was time to buy things at the shop. He also told me that if you tried fighting with the staff or other patients they locked you in isolation where you didn't get out to smoke or interact with the other patients. He told me the biggest mistake one can make in Sterkfontein is to refuse medication. He then introduced me to all the other patients. All the patients in Sterkfontein liked and respected Mike. Some even called him Baba.

Everybody wanted to go home; even I missed my family. I wished I could go back home to KwaZulu-Natal. I didn't care about my life under the bridge anymore, about the drugs and the 'thing' I couldn't speak about to anyone. I wanted to go home to my real family. Life at Sterkfontein was hard. We had to wake up at 7:00 and make our beds, bath and have breakfast at 8:30 or 9:00. We could smoke in the hall because we were not allowed to go outdoors. We were locked in the hall or the TV room during the day and were not allowed to go to bed during the day so our rooms were kept locked. After breakfast we would sit on the chairs and chat. Some folks killed time while waiting for lunch by bullying others. Some patients were really crazy, some were better than others and some were okay.

Nurse Mike cared for us more than any other nurse in Sterkfontein. He had a class where he taught us about mental illnesses and the dangers of drug and alcohol abuse. He helped patients to learn how to use computers and sometimes played us movies and music on his laptop. Staff Nurse Mike made Sterkfontein a lot less depressing. It was always chaos when Nurse Mike was off-duty. Patients used to fight a lot and make noise, or pee on the floor just to give the nurses a headache. No other nurse did what Nurse Mike did for his patients and no one respected them like he did. Most of the other nurses in Sterkfontein treated patients like they were crazy, useless people or only respected patients from rich families who had regular visitors. Some patients had been there for more than nine months and had never been visited. Some didn't have relatives, and nobody visited the others that did because of what they'd done back home.

Dr Skhosana was another angel trying her best to make Sterkfontein a better place. She was sweet and friendly and cared about her patients just like Nurse Mike did. I stayed in Sterkfontein for two months and 2 weeks because she wanted to get to know me better and didn't discharge me. She wanted to know if I was telling her the truth and was the first person to discover that I was homeless. I liked and trusted her, not only because she was attractive but also because she was friendly. She made me feel like I was the only patient in her files and that my secrets were safe with her.

She asked me if I had any friends or family members who knew where I was. I remembered that I had a few friends' contact numbers in my small dirty notebook in which I used to write about my experiences out there on the streets. It was in my bag in the storage room, so she sent a nurse to fetch it. She wanted to call my friends to see if anyone cared enough to come and visit me. Most of them were homeless so they didn't have cell phones or care whether I was dead or alive, so I could only rely on those friends who helped me with book donations. I didn't give her my mother's number either because I didn't want my family to know about the life that I was living. I didn't want my dear mother and my brothers to know that I had turned into a struggling, suicidal, homeless man in Johannesburg.

Dr Skhosana began calling all the contacts I gave her. Fortunately one Good Samaritan did care about me, my good friend Ken Nortje. Ken was, and still is, a managing director of a company called Malnor Publications. He and his business partner helped me a lot while I was in Sterkfontein and after I got discharged. He asked Dr Skhosana how she thought they could help me, so she told him that I needed support because I didn't have proper accommodation outside. She arranged for him to come and visit me. He brought me a lot of snacks to eat, some toiletries and new clothes to wear when I got discharged. Dr Skhosana met Ken and told him that I was homeless; he offered to pay my rent for a few months until I was able to stand on my own two feet again. That was the best news ever; I was now looking forward to being discharged and starting over again. A few weeks later Dr Skhosana said she thought I was ready to face the world outside again.

In Sterkfontein patients don't just get discharged every day, so Nurse Mike and most patients were very happy for me. He decided to throw a little snack party for me and we had a good time. Not everybody took the news so well though and Mbongeni, who had been in Sterkfontein for more than ten months, really didn't take the news well at all. He started fighting and breaking windows and wanted to know why a guy who had only been there for two months and 2 weeks was already going home when he had been locked up for more than ten months. He accused the doctors of being corrupt, saying he was not crazy and that they were. I was told not to feel bad because apparently he didn't like it when anybody was discharged. He was given an injection to calm him down and then he was taken to the isolation ward.

I wanted to continue being clean of drugs and I was proud that I was able to go without for that long. It was a great achievement. It made me felt good. I wanted to do more with my life. And I did do my bit to make the world a better place as this was the time my reading club was born.

I couldn't sleep that night for thinking about how I was going to change my life in the outside world. I was proud that I could go without drugs for so long – I had been in Sterkfontein for two months and two weeks – and that achievement made me feel good. I wanted to do more with my life. In the morning, when the nurse knocked, I was already up and my bed was made. Excitement was written on my face because being discharged from Sterkfontein felt like walking out of prison.

Qala kabusha: Trying to make a new start

BEFORE BREAKFAST WAS SERVED, a driver was already outside waiting to take me to Mr Kenneth Nortje's office in Auckland Park. The driver didn't talk much, except to ask if I had everything that I needed. I didn't have a lot to take with me, just my book bag and my shirt and jeans, since his boss, had bought me new clothes to wear. It was a long drive from Sterkfontein to Auckland Park. Mr Nortje had already told them about me and when we arrived at the Malnor Publications building people were happy to see me. As we walked up to his office where his partner was waiting he told me never again to do such a stupid thing like trying to take my own life just because I have problems.

Mr Nortje and his partner both promised they'd help me as much as they could and asked how much I thought I would need for rent. I said maybe a thousand rand or a little bit more than that. I was not looking for anything fancy. I just needed a roof over my head. They gave me R1800 and told me to call if I needed anything more. They knew that for a street-wise guy like me it wouldn't be a problem to find a room or a space to rent, and Mr Nortje said I should come back to the office if I didn't find a place. They asked a driver to drop me off at Jozi central where I could look for a room to rent.

I knew my way around town and I knew where to find a place to rent. I went to a building called Central Park in Joubert Park and asked the security guard at the reception if there was a room or a space available to rent. The good news was that they had plenty and he told me to knock at room number 1102 because the tenant was looking for people to share a space there. The room was on the 11th floor, and the elevator was broken but none of that mattered to me. I needed a roof over my head, not an elevator. I knocked on the door. An old lady opened the door and greeted me with a smile on her face. I introduced myself and I told her that I was looking for a space to rent. The space that was available was in the lounge, which she had divided with curtains into three spaces big enough to fit a bed. Since I didn't even have a bed, I told her I would take the space. My monthly rental would be R550, excluding electricity.

I didn't mind because I would still be left with enough change to take care of my other needs. I paid her the rent, then went to the Indian-owned shop to buy a sponge, a blanket, a pillow, and some food to eat. I asked two kids to help me take my belongings up to the 11th floor and for that they charged me a fee of R20. They knew that I couldn't carry my sponge, pillow, blanket and my plastic grocery bag up to the 11th floor on my own, so they told me to forget about negotiating their charge. When they saw the bag of books on the floor in my space they wanted to know what the books were about. Since I like books so much I was very interested in their hunger for knowledge. I like people who are interested in books, especially if they are young and can drop everything to read a new book. I paid them their fee and gave them each a book as bonus gifts. They liked them so much that they came back for more books to read the following day. Even if I didn't know it at the time my readers' club was born right there with only two wise kids as the first members. I didn't know anyone else in the building so those kids became my friends from day one.

I had decided to carry on doing what I do best, which is connecting with my customers and selling books. When I got to Empire Road the next morning I was surprised to see how much things had changed. My friend Siyabonga was still there, doing what he did best – selling pity (or you can call it begging), but there were new faces there that day. He told me these new faces were now free to sell and beg and wash car windows at Empire Road because the bully Bongani was killed in a fight – he had been stabbed in the neck while fighting for ownership of that street corner and had died instantly. While this was sad news, I didn't know anyone else who would choose to die for a

street corner. Where's the honour in dying for a begging spot?
Yet many brothers die for stupid reasons. Bongani died young
to prove that he was the street king of Empire Road.

Remember I told you that I didn't fight back when Bongani
forced me to wait under the tree for him to finish begging?
If I had fought back, perhaps it would be me who was dead,
killed by Bongani for a begging spot at Empire Road. Today
he is history but I'm still here telling you about his sad death.
I'm still here because of what I learned at a very young age:
cowards live longer, and never argue with a fool.

One day I met a lady who later became a friend of mine.
Her name is Beverly Crooks. She used to see me selling books
at Empire Road when she dropped her son at Wits University.
Then one day she parked under the bridge and called me over.
She told me about the Herbalife World of Opportunities and
the Herbalife distributing business. It sounded like a cool
idea. I thought about all the old people when I was a carer in
old age homes years before who would buy those nutritional
products she showed me. I thought I'd make a fortune out of
being a Herbalife distributor. I was sold even before she finished
explaining everything to me. When she told me about the cost
of a start-up kit, I was so excited I didn't tell her that I didn't
have the money – I knew that my friends at Malnor Publications
trusted and believed in me. I called them and explained the whole
Herbalife thing and asked for a R1000 loan – not to give to me
but to put in Beverly's bank account. They deposited the money
and the following morning Beverly brought me my start-up kit.

There's nothing much more to tell about my Herbalife
business except that it was a flop. I failed to get customers and

I was very quick to give up, probably because I never had to pay for it and we all know that if you never paid for something, you don't pay attention.

Still, my life was improving. I felt good. I felt I had a chance to regain what I had lost.

I now had a place to go home to, there was always food on my table even if I slept late and didn't go sell books. My life was much better than when I lived under the bridge but I missed my friends; I missed getting high and forgetting all the worries, struggles and challenges that come with being alive.

I admit I was lucky when God gave me a second and a third chance. But I blew them all.

I went for some dope after three months of being clean and then there was no turning back. I took my friend Siyabonga up to Hillbrow to surprise him with some good stuff that we both liked to smoke while I was still a junkie. I burned all the bridges with my friends who were helping me with my rental payments and with my landlord, but fortunately not with my friends who I used to sleep with under the bridge. I still had a place to call home since they still had my clothes they'd taken as a rental payment while I was still new on the streets.

So there I was, once again, with nothing left but a blanket and a few clothes and a bagful of books. My friends welcomed me with open arms; they didn't like it when one of us made it out. They used to say 'you can take a street kid out of the streets but you can never take the streets out of him'. It felt like an accurate description of who I had become.

Now that I was back, words like 'I told you so' were often thrown at me. And it did hurt a lot – I felt ashamed and humiliated by my failure. I even started believing that I was bewitched. Regrets always come later, right? Now that I was back there was nothing glamorous about being on the streets again and I wished I were still living in that space that my friends had so kindly rented for me at Central Park. But when I had it I wanted to be homeless again! I just didn't know what I wanted. Drugs were driving me crazy. Sometimes I blamed God for creating me. Sometimes I thanked God for saving my life when I tried to kill myself. The truth is I was alive but didn't know what I was living for. I had lost my job, forgotten my family and lost everything I ever worked for and cared about.

I was homeless the first time because I didn't have a choice, or at least that was what I thought. I was homeless because I was a drug addict and an alcoholic and had lost my job. I had tried to kill myself to escape my life but survived and been given a second chance. Those were the reasons I had become homeless but now I had no excuses. Now I was homeless out of choice because I missed being homeless! I had been offered a fresh start and been given a roof over my head but I chose instead to go live under the bridge again and smoke drugs instead.

This time I had given up on life completely. I was just like any other homeless person: not caring about my oral hygiene, not bathing. I didn't care what people thought or said about me or even about being alive. I didn't care about my collectable first-edition books. All I knew was how to hustle from the pavement and tell people in their cars about my books. Every cent I made I used to buy more drugs. I couldn't care less about my life.

I lived like this for many months, almost a year, until one day I found something that helped me change my ways for good. I started reading a book entitled *A Purpose Driven Life* by Rick Warren. I know I'll be thinking about that book until the day I die. It had the answers to my questions about why I was alive, whether my life matters and what on earth am I here for. That book helped me to get closer to God and to value my life beyond survival on the streets. I wanted to improve my life, and be happy like God planned life for us. After reading that book I knew I had to change. Then I bought a novel called *Sophie's World* by Jostein Gaarder.

Sophie Amundsen is fourteen years old, when the book begins, living in Norway. She begins a strange correspondence course in philosophy. Every day, a letter comes to her mailbox that contains a few questions and then later in the day a package comes with some typed pages describing the ideas of a philosopher who dealt with the issues raised by the questions. Although at first she does not know, later on Sophie learns that Alberto Knox is the name of the philosopher who is teaching her. He sends her packages via his dog Hermes. Alberto first tells Sophie that philosophy is extremely relevant to life and that if we don't question and ponder our very existence we aren't really living. Then he proceeds to go through the history of Western philosophy. Alberto teaches Sophie about the ancient myths that people had in the days before they tried to come up with natural explanations for the processes in the world. Then she learns about the natural philosophers who were concerned with change. Next Alberto describes Democritus and the theory of indivisible atoms underlying all of nature as well as the concept of fate.

But I digress with this paraphrasing of Sophie's story. The point is, Sophie's story helped me win myself back because I learned that if we don't question and think about our existence then we aren't really living. After that, I only read self-help manuals. I read many different authors like Joseph Prince, Dr JC Maxwell, TD Jakes, Fredrick K Mamabolo, Erwin W Lutzer, Henry Blackaby and many others who write books that make you want to be a better person. I believe that they helped me become something better than I was.

I told my friends under the bridge that I had lived without drugs for more than two months in Sterkfontein Psychiatric Hospital and I didn't die, so we could all win the war against that killer addiction. They laughed, saying that if I had won, why I was going back to living under the bridge with them. I won't lie, those words hurt, not just a bit – they hurt me so much that they fuelled my desire to keep going for days without smoking. Books were my new drugs and I was really addicted. Most of the guys I lived under the bridge with were bullies and dream crushers. If I listened to all the things they were saying, I would still be living under the bridge, smoking rocks or possibly be as dead as most of them are today. Instead I chose to listen to what my books were telling me, that nothing is impossible.

Like I already mentioned, I'm not a saint, but I do go to church and I believe in God. It also makes me happy to share what little I have with others, no matter what it is. That's how I was raised. My mother used to say giving is a gift for the giver and that we should give so we can receive. I used my mom's advice and started a feeding scheme by sharing what little I had with my brothers who lived under the Nelson Mandela

Bridge with me. After selling my books every day I went to the shop with the money I made and bought packs of soup and loaves of bread for them to eat in the morning before we went to hustle. I know drug addicts only care about getting high so they buy drugs then wake up hungry in the morning and look for food in the trash bins all over the city of Johannesburg. At first they laughed at me and called me *Father Theresa*, but the truth was that they liked what I was doing. I was happy that I was making a difference with the money I could've been wasting on drugs. I'd rather be the one making people smile than the one everyone laughed at.

My idea was a success. Friends from other street corners began visiting us for a cup of soup and four slices of bread before going to hustle in the mornings. My bread and soup become as famous as any drug. Now that I was off the drugs I was able to save some money for my other needs. My friend Henry, who was a bartender at a local club called Emashanganeni, used to keep the money for me.

Then I met a young man who was a student at the university. His name is Peter Walters. He used to drive past me on his way to Wits and when the traffic light turned red I would get lucky and I could talk to him about books. Every time he stopped I smiled because he always paid R100 for any book he liked. Meeting Peter Walters was a blessing. He was a paying customer with a golden heart. He is like a brother to me. One morning he gave me a letter telling me that he was about to graduate from Wits University, and that he'd like to help me with a contribution of R1000 each month. When I first read that letter I couldn't believe my eyes. Never before had I heard of a young man offering to help a stranger on the street with a percentage of his first salary. To me, Peter Walters was heaven sent. I simply had to wait for him to get a job and get paid his first salary. Peter had faith in me because he wrote me that letter before he even had a job. This time I wanted to prove that people's faith in me was justified. I had already been clean for more than 9 months. In the eyes of my homeless friends I was a champion because I gave up drugs when everybody said I'd never be able to do it after relapsing after being clean for more than two months and losing my pride and accommodation again.

You'd be surprised to know that it has been more than two years since that letter and Peter Walters still sends me that R1000 every month.

The return of the
Pavement Bookworm

GOD ENJOYED BLESSING ME just as much as I enjoyed blessing others. He kept showering me with blessing after blessing, which made me realise that givers really never lack. One afternoon, I was waiting for a customer to come out from the university and get his book, so I could give my friend Henry some money to keep for me. I was sitting on the pavement reading *The Da Vinci Code* by Dan Brown. My pile of books was as nicely organised as always so if I stood up I could lift them up neatly and continue selling. I wasn't really enjoying the book but couldn't stop reading. I thought the author had something against Christianity and I wanted to know what that was. The story was about a mysterious world of conspiracy and secret codes, and some historical documents that had been hidden for many centuries by the church. I got hooked from the first page. While I was reading, a guy came towards me with a big smile on his face, and a big digital camera in his hands.

He greeted me and asked, 'My brother, what made you decide to come sit on the pavement in the middle of the road and read *The Da Vinci Code?*'

He still had a smile on his face and seemed very kind and I prayed to God that the guys didn't show up because I knew they would take something from him, either his camera or his wallet.

'My good brother, what you see here is a mobile bookshop, not just a guy who got bored and decided to sit in the middle of the street with a pile of books and read,' I replied.

He asked what books I was selling and how much I charge for each book. I told him that my books don't all cost the same because I value a book according to how good it is. Then I gave him the synopsis of a few books I had in my pile. He was very impressed and asked if it was okay if he made a video of me telling him about my books and a little bit more about myself, like who I was, where I was from and what made me sell books on the street. I thought, why not? In Sir Richard Branson's book *Screw It Let's Do It* he liked trying new things and he liked having fun. I was having fun sharing my story and telling him about my books. I always liked telling people about books.

I never intended to be the Pavement Bookworm when I did that video interview with Mr Tebogo Malope. I didn't know that an ordinary young dark-skinned man like me had a means to share my story with the world, or that Mr Malope would change my life with the simple two-minute video clip he made. What I had in mind was that he would make this video clip and play it for some township boys. Maybe they could learn a thing or two about drug abuse from my experience, and maybe they'd learn from my stupid mistakes and want to quit just like I did. Remember, when Tebogo made that video I was already victorious over drug addiction.

I was a champion to my homeless friends because I used the same money we would've wasted on drugs together to do something for everybody's benefit. Everyone was benefiting from my book sales. I bought soup and bread for all of us and gave the rest of the money to Henry to keep for me. But some guys hated me for what I was doing and called me names, saying that I thought that I was someone. They suffered from a syndrome known as PHD (Pull Him Down). They'd liked me, though, when they thought that we were all in it together and that drugs would kill us all.

Although it was only nine months since I had stopped doing drugs I had gone a long way in the fight against drug abuse. Many of my customers at Empire remember how hard I was trying; I even asked them to buy tablets called *Super Tags* to cure people who wanted to quit but were afraid of the symptoms, side effects and cravings caused by withdrawal from the drugs. It was not easy but some people bought us a few bottles of *Super Tags* at R500 a box. I wouldn't say we failed because three guys were able to stop, admittedly two of them relapsed but one is still clean as I'm telling this story to you today.

After my video interview with Tebogo Malope went viral on the internet, things turned messy. Everybody wanted to know who I was and if the so-called Pavement Bookworm really existed or if it was just another work of fiction. Media people from TV and newspapers came to visit me on Empire Road to follow up on the story.

I was in every newspaper; even ones I didn't know existed. Radio stations invited me for studio interviews and I received a lot of gifts. I was getting a lot of book gifts too and I didn't know where to keep them. When Henry saw my story in the newspaper he did not only keep money safe for me, he started keeping the books too. People of all races and classes visited me and even people who used to ignore me started smiling and wanting to know more about me.

Once again I had a choice about whether to sleep in a cheap hotel or camp with my buddies under the Nelson Mandela Bridge. The publicity one video clip gave me is the media attention that many celebrities seek and will do all sorts of things to get. Many companies pay loads of money for the advertising my mobile bookshop was getting. I made friends with authors who came to visit me to give me their book gifts. I was making money but it was hard to get off the streets because my brothers depended on me for their morning soup and bread. I was the only homeless man I knew with a Twitter account and a Facebook page, and my phone began ringing non-stop.

By the end of 2012, I had made enough money to go and visit my family in KwaZulu-Natal after many years. They knew that I was still alive because the Pavement Bookworm was doing the rounds in the media. At least I didn't have to tell them my story.

I bought everything brand new from head to toe and some gifts for uMa and my brothers. I still had uMa's contact number but I didn't call because I wanted to surprise them. After travelling for more than seven hundred kilometres crammed in a taxi we arrived at my beautiful hometown of Port Shepstone. I took another taxi to Oshabeni where my home is.

It felt good being home again. My mother was happy to see me. My family had some questions for me – Where had I been? How had it been? Why it had been so long since I had made contact or sent money? Some asked if I had missed them. It was very emotional. People were very happy to see me again – even those who used to gossip about when I got stabbed, dropped out of school and tried to kill myself and called me a loser and a bad influence and *nsangwini* (weed addict). All was forgotten; it was like it never happened. It felt like I had a new body. My holiday was not very long because the City of Gold was calling me back, I had more dreams and they were bigger than the small town Oshabeni. If I wanted my dreams to come true I had to go back to the gold digger's city. Look at this book you're reading; it is one of my dreams.

I didn't need to pack because I lived like a rat in Johannesburg. I took a bus from Oslo Beach that arrived at 5:30 am at Park Station in Johannesburg. I waited in the waiting area for the sun to rise and then went to get a few books from Henry's place. On my way I received a call from a lady called Thenji Stamela who works for a morning show called *Expresso* on SABC 3. They wanted to do an interview with the Pavement Bookworm. I gave her the green light and she said she'd meet me at Empire Road with her crew at 9:30 am the next morning. I was early as usual and arranged my books neatly. I started selling books while I waited for Thenji and her *Expresso* crew to show up. What I didn't know was that the media attention had turned my friends sour.

My own boys, my friends who lived under the bridge with me, came in numbers with new faces to attack me. They were led by Simon, popularly known as Lesiba – another heartless street king. After Bongani was stabbed to death, Simon replaced him. It was like the devil sent him to give me a hard time. He never liked me and he said I thought I was better than everyone else since I managed to quit drugs successfully. He expected me to relapse again and when that didn't happen he started abusing me every day, calling my feeding scheme a Mickey Mouse business. He physically attacked me many times but I never fought back because he was expecting it, and then he would kill me with the okapi knife he kept in his pocket. I still have scars on my head, which are reminders of how he once broke a bottle on my head.

As soon as Thenji and the crew arrived it was like a tsunami. The cameraman was setting up his camera while Thenji was busy introducing herself. I couldn't believe what happened next and that I got to live and didn't die that day. Simon started beating me and said he was going to kill me because I kept on calling the media people to come annoy them with their big cameras. He claimed that he knew that the video they were about to make was going be shown on TV to show their families and friends where they were hiding. They said I was embarrassing them. They never wanted to see me again. They told me that if they saw me on Empire Road or at the Mandela Bridge again they would skin me alive. Simon said he would be more than happy to 'personally organise my trip to hell'. I believed him.

The camera man tried to explain that they were only going to interview me and only tell my story and video me. But the guys didn't understand his explanation and it only made things worse and they carried on beating me. Everyone ran for their lives and the crew gave me a ride in their car and dropped me off far away from the *nyaope* guys.

The interview didn't happen that day, and from then on I was no longer welcome on Empire Road. Hate drove Simon to turn it into a no-go zone for me. Since I was forcefully removed I knew if they ever saw me there I would die like Bongani. Since that day I have never stepped foot there again. Things had turned sour once again; I didn't know where to go from there. Mandela Bridge was my home and Empire Road was paying my bills. Without both those things I had to start all over again.

Fortunately my good friend Henry introduced me to a friend who had a friend who had cheap accommodation to rent. Henry paid my first month's rent because I had used all the money I had saved to travel to KwaZulu-Natal. There was nothing sexy about my new home. We lived in an abandoned building with no electricity or running water. The only good thing about it was that I only had to pay R100 as monthly rent and I didn't have to worry about a bed or a blanket because my landlord was kind enough to share his bed with me.

It helps having good friends like Henry, but he was not going to feed me. I had to make my own money and take care of myself. My problem was that I was used to being my own boss, I didn't like the idea of working for somebody else. Even if I wanted to go job hunting it was a big joke because I had lost my Identity Document and I had no Curriculum Vitae or a reference from a previous employer. I had many books that I could've sold but I didn't know where to sell them. The people from Wits University were my friends and they supported me. I missed them. I wanted to go back there but I knew my friends-turned-enemies would murder me. Since I stopped doing drugs I valued my life more than money and, although some people from Wits still owed me money, I was afraid to go back.

I love God. He did a good job by creating the lucky fool I am. That day he proved to me just how much he loved and cared about me. My friend Peter Walters called to tell me we had to meet in Greenside because he wanted to give me my share of his first salary. I didn't know where Greenside was and he said to take a taxi to Randburg and ask the driver to drop me off at a restaurant called Doppio Zero. I did as instructed and when I got there he was already waiting. We had lunch at Doppio Zero then we went to an ATM where he withdrew R1000 for me. He showed me around Greenside and it was peaceful and quiet there that day and I liked that place. I only saw a man in his seventies begging. I knew an old man like him was not doing *nyaope* so I didn't expect any trouble. The following day I packed my books and took a taxi to Greenside. I chose Gleneagles Road.

Many people knew about my famous pile of books and me. They didn't waste time and started supporting me right away.

There were a few rotten potatoes that looked at me like I was crazy and made racist comments. They didn't know that I had seen and heard worse. I just didn't care. I looked at them like 'hey fool, do you even know who I am?' and continued doing my thing. I made some cash, had lunch at a nice restaurant and took some cash home. I fell in love with Greenside from day one.

The thing that broke my heart was that every day on my way to Greenside, the taxi went via Empire Road and I would see the guys who forced me to leave my street corner and my friends from Wits. They still did everything they used to do when I lived on the streets with them, begging for money and smoking it up and then getting back on the streets to beg for more – a monkey's game. Some hadn't bathed for a year or two and I don't know where all the others went but I knew that some were dead or doing time in jail. They were gambling with their lives. They saw their friends dying every day but continued doing drugs while waiting for their turn to die, like the guy who has sex with a girl who tells him 'Hey Mister, I'm HIV positive' and he says, 'Liar! How can a beautiful lady like you be HIV positive?' When HIV becomes AIDS and he gets sick he says, 'Silly me, what was I thinking? She told me but I was blinded by her beauty.' Drug addicts know that drugs will kill them but only regret it when it's too late to turn back.

I was making some money in Greenside, but it didn't make me happy because I was used to making people smile. I suppose I could've started another feeding scheme but my black brothers had broken my heart when they showed me how ungrateful people can be. After all the things I had done for them they still didn't like seeing things going well for me. So I decided to invest in our future leaders instead, not that I was making a fortune, but I saw myself as blessed for surviving what I had survived. One of the many things I have learnt is that while you can fast and pray or go to church and pray as a way to thank God, there's no better way to thank God than by doing things for others. I realised that I didn't have to wait until all my prayers were all answered. I did not need to wait until I had more than I needed; anyone can start by sharing the little you already have. I often hear rich kids saying 'poverty is contagious'. Well, that's bull. Don't wait until you're rich to change the world; start with what you can do today. God will prove to you that givers never lack. I decided that no matter how little I was making I would share with others. My mother taught me that giving is a gift to the giver; so when I need a gift I give somebody a gift. You won't be poor when you give a hungry kid some food to eat or a homeless man some clothes to wear. You see, good reader, happiness is the gift I get from giving and it is highly contagious … as contagious as a smile is.

Building a happy sandpit: My book club takes off

REMEMBER I ALREADY TOLD YOU that the two kids who carried my parcels for me in the Central Park apartment when I first came out of Sterkfontein were the first members of my book readers' club? Well, I asked them to meet me at Joubert Park with their friends one day after school. We made more friends in the park and every day new friends came to join us. Our family started growing rapidly, even though some kids took our books and never came back. The kids told their friends, their friends liked the idea and they invited their friends. Our club was growing. We were growing faster than I could make the money to buy more children's books for our club, so I asked my customers to exchange as many children's books as they could for a single adult's book. They brought lots of children's books to exchange. Most simply donated and took nothing in exchange. That's how we grew from those first two members to having more than 50 members by the time I did my TEDx talk. We are growing stronger every day and we have more than 250 kids in downtown Johannesburg under our wings, all interested in books. Do yourselves a favour: next time you are anywhere near Joubert Park, ask any kid you see about the uncle that gives them books. Their answers will be proof of the impact that The Pavement Bookworm has made in many of their lives.

Greenside took longer than I had hoped to fall in love with the Pavement Bookworm, but I had fallen in love with Greenside and needed to find a way to make it work. Yes, people were buying my books but I needed more customers. So I decided to make my new spot just as famous as my old spot at Empire Road. I called the guys from SABC 3's breakfast show *Expresso* to do the interview we didn't do on Empire Road. That interview worked like magic because after the interview aired more people came to buy books from me.

Maybe I was getting greedy because I was still not satisfied. I needed more customers. I received a call from the producer of *Jenny's Book Show* on Talk Radio 702, saying they were interested in doing an interview with me. As I needed more free advertising for my new spot in Greenside I grabbed the opportunity and gave her the green light. It was a smart move because the Pavement Bookworm was introduced to more new friends.

One of them was DJ Sbu, a famous South African DJ. He really is a man with a golden heart and he played a big role in the life of the Pavement Bookworm. DJ Sbu got hold of me and asked me to do an interview on his show on Metro FM. After that our friendship grew from strength to strength. After the interview he called and said he'd like to help pay my expenses so I could re-write my Grade 12 and help grow my readers' club. Every day was a good day for me from then on. He gave me more media exposure and introduced me to famous people and powerful entrepreneurs. One day he interviewed me on the same day that he interviewed a gentleman named Colin J Browne, the author of the book *How to Build a Happy Sandpit*. It teaches entrepreneurs how to hire the right man for the job and how to make the people who work for you more productive and happy at work. What can I say about Mr Browne other than that this world needs more people like him and that we're still friends today. That cool cat gave me the gift of a VIP ticket to attend the Global Success Summit, an event held at Sandton Convention Centre where he was one of the speakers. The summit was packed with rich people, business minds and movers and shakers. I was the 'poorest' guy who attended that event – I didn't even have a bank account. This didn't stop the Pavement Bookworm from mingling with the rich and famous and it was a great experience.

Introducing me to Mr Browne wasn't the only thing that the legendary DJ Sbu did for the Pavement Bookworm. He didn't like the place where I lived. Although I had a roof over my head he thought it was too dangerous for me there and that it was only slightly better from being a street kid. I was getting robbed and once I got stabbed while a robbery was in progress.

Just like his name Sibusiso, DJ Sbu was a real blessing to me. He paid my lodgings at Johannesburger Hotel on Twist Street, just to keep me safe and away from thugs. He also wanted to find me accommodation near a school where I could go to complete my Grade 12. DJ Sbu did not give up easily and he worked hard to get me enrolled. Rental can get expensive, so he took me into his home to live with him and his wife and their daughter.

Through DJ Sbu, I got a glimpse of the good life. He bought me fresh clothes and food and new books. He helped me get a new Identity Document and managed to get me into a school and a place to live. We used to travel together visiting schools and doing motivational talks. Life was good.

For some reason, as soon as things were going my way things fell apart. I never really started school but I went to collect stationery and got my accommodation sorted. My granny passed away and uMa got sick so I had to go home for a few days. When I got home there was more family drama and problems. My head was messed up. I decided that my family was more important than flashy material things and school, all of which had to wait. My mother was there for me when we had nothing to eat and comforted me when malnutrition had ravaged my body. The least I could do was to be supportive to her; I was home for two months. Even though DJ Sbu had already spent a lot more than R15 000 on me I had to drop everything and rush back to KwaZulu-Natal; but he never gave up on me. He is still my good friend and is still very supportive.

Next year I will go and write my Grade 12 again and he is behind me all the way. What I like about him is that he doesn't just talk the talk. This year he is back at his desk doing his MBA. I know that young black South Africans who make things happen like DJ Sbu will always be an inspiration to me.

The unluckiest lucky guy I know

I GREW UP WATCHING MY MOTHER being kind to people that weren't always grateful. But I am testament to what kindness from strangers can do to change your life. I have had people who didn't have to help me go out of their way to help me. I'm afraid that this book will be as thick as a dictionary if I go into the details about how good people like Peter Walters have been to me. Not only did he have faith in me and give me R1000 a month from his first salary, he introduced me to my new family, the Bryanston Bible Church. I'm the luckiest unlucky guy I know because every time I pray to God my prayers always get answered. After each prayer is answered another challenge comes my way. Through my journey I have come to know and make friends with a number of really incredible people from all walks of life, and I have developed friendships that overlook racial lines. I value them all because they add value to my life and I learn something new every time I'm with them. What I like most about them is they make me smile when I felt like giving up.

I continue to be amazed at the power of family. Even after the many years I spent without them, I love my family just as much as you love yours. We've been through a lot together; from having an abusive father to almost being killed by his crazy family members to no Christmas lunch; no fireworks to celebrate New Year's like all the families in my hood always do to no money for taxi fare to go to the beach like all other kids do when celebrating first of January of every year in coastal KwaZulu-Natal. We lost many loved ones – our relatives and family members who we cried and laughed together with. I have been away from home for a very long time and only go home for family emergencies or for Christmas holidays. Yet, these are the people that know and understand me better than people who I spend almost the whole year with in Johannesburg. All the memories we made together, all the hard times we've been through, all the tears we shared and the situations we survived, money can't buy all that.

What I have seen and learned is that everybody wants to be successful; even a hobo wants to be successful. What I also learned is that success means different things to different people. To most people success means wealth, but to some it means recognition, while to some it means happiness, satisfaction and peace of mind. I know for sure that success requires sacrifice.

One day DJ Sbu, PJ Speaker, another gentleman called

Frederick K Mamabdo and I were speaking to the youth in Tembisa. All the words Frederick spoke to the youth were filled with wisdom. I was very impressed with what he had to say.

'Sir, your words are filled with wisdom. Can I please ask you something?' I said to him.

'Why not?' he said.

'Cool! Tell me your definition of success?' I asked.

'Success is when one sets goals and progressively accomplishes them. Look at these definitions carefully, "Progressive" means that success is a journey, not a destination. We never arrive; after we have reached one goal, we go on the next and the next and the next. "Accomplish" means it is an experience. Outside forces cannot make me feel successful. I have to feel it within myself. It is internal not external. Mr Philani, success and happiness go hand in hand. Success is getting what you want and happiness is wanting what you've got! Existence alone is not success. Success is a lot more than just existence,' he explained.

I would've loved to learn more from him, but time was against us. DJ Sbu had to go do his radio show at Metro FM but I learned a lot that day from that wise man.

The media introduced me to many people and opportunities. I don't remember if that insert was shown on eTV News or on ANN7. All I remember is that the creative director from a marketing agency called Gullan and Gullan was watching an insert about me and she liked my story and said that they wanted to do something to help me. That lovely lady with a golden heart is Desiree Gullan. She sent Kathryn McConnachie to arrange a meeting with me. Kathryn followed me on Twitter and sent me a tweet saying, '*Hi Philani. I'd like us to meet.*

My directors would like to help you take your project to the next level.'

We arranged our meeting via Twitter, messaging each other. Two weeks and four days later we met for the first time at my favourite restaurant, Doppio Zero in Greenside. People call it my office because every time I have to meet someone we meet there. That meeting was the beginning of many good things. Kath asked me what I wanted help with. I told her that I really appreciated that they were so interested in helping me grow as an individual but the only thing I needed from them was for them to help me help my kids. She asked me how they could do that and who my kids were. So I told her about my family of children in Joubert Park and the kids readers' club. I told her everything she wanted to know, like how many kids were members of my club, their ages, what grades they were doing at school and if they had parents or not. The more I explained about the kids' living conditions the more she understood why I cared so much about them more than I cared about my own needs.

Finally, she asked me a question that I was praying she would ask. She asked what my kids needed the most. In those days the kids needed stationery and our club needed new books to read. I had many friends on social platforms like Facebook and Twitter who wanted to send me books but it wasn't easy because many were in foreign countries like China, the UK and the USA. They wanted to help with book donations but it was hard for them to get the books.

I told her about my friend Dean, who had agreed to pay someone to design a website for me, so that I could communicate with all the people who wanted to help. It would be easy for people to get to know more about the readers' club, my kids and their needs and how to get involved if I had a website. She said it would be a pleasure for the Gullan and Gullan team to design a website for me and also to help with storage space when people sent books. That's how The Pavement Bookworm Foundation – www.pavementbookworm.co.za – was born.

While my website was under construction, Kathryn worked extra hard transporting me to and from the office every time I had to be there. She made sure my website looked just the way I wanted it to look. She is head of copy and content at Gullan and Gullan but she spent her time working on making my dream a reality. I guess everybody at Gullan and Gullan believed in me and that's why they invested so much time and resources to make sure that my site happened and that I was satisfied with it. Even though Dean Lotter had offered to pay the bill – I never paid them a dime – they made me feel like I was a paying customer. I was there to give the nod or reject what I was not cool with.

I wanted my website to be extra special so we decided to launch it with a bang on 18 July 2014, which is International Nelson Mandela Day, in Joubert Park. All the members from the readers' club, the team from Gullan and Gullan and friends were there. They bought the children freshly made lunch and drinks; Staedtler blessed them with a stationery donation. Gifted Young Leaders and Philips were there. All thanks to the donation that my friend Dean Lotter made. Oh yes, my kids had more than enough books to read since many South Africans showed us love. Although I don't have enough words to thank everybody who contributed I'm grateful from the bottom of my heart.

My website launched with a bang and we didn't just do 67

minutes on Mandela Day. My kids still use the stationery and now they do their homework at night, though they live in a building with no electricity, because they still have those solar lights courtesy of Dean Lotter and Phillips. They still read the books they received on Mandela Day.

I have so many reasons to be proud that I'm alive; I don't need anyone to remind me. I don't live just to exist; I live to make a difference. If I die today I'll rest in peace knowing that I played my part; I touched many lives and left my mark. I do what I do not because anyone is watching or for public display but to make me happy. A smile is highly contagious and every time I make someone smile, it makes me smile too. Even a child knows that the ugliest guy in the world looks so much better when he smiles.

Through my observations, I think money is as highly addictive as *nyaope*; chasing money is gambling with your life just as much as experimenting with drugs is. Money makes people heartless just like drugs can turn the sweetest kid into a heartless criminal. Money makers are like drug addicts; once they get some they want more, once they get more, they want more and more of it, once they get more and more, they want more and more and more at any expense. They'll risk their lives to get more, and what's this stupid phrase they use? Oh they call it *get rich or die trying*. I mean that's stupid, right? Why would you risk your life for something that you've already seen so many people die for? For something that you have seen many people making more than too much of it, but have died and left it here in the world where they found it? If you're still struggling to answer that one I've got an answer: stupidity. Money makes people so stupid they forget about what really matters in life.

A country of my skull

I STARTED DOCUMENTING MY LIFE on the street, writing everything on a notebook that I kept with me at all times. But life became easier when my friend, Linda Wilson, gave me a laptop, which I used to record my story. But unfortunately I lost most parts of this book in one incident. I was attacked and robbed by three men and from their accent it sounded like they might have been from Zimbabwe.

I was walking on Leyds Street, heading to where I used to go to collect my book club kids from the park where they played soccer, close to Royal Park Hotel, when this guy came toward me from behind and held me by the neck and as suddenly as he appeared two more appeared and started picking my pockets. They were doing it in a way that told me they wanted to make sure they left nothing behind. The laptop they took contained a better version of this story.

After some time and some digging, my friend, Brian and I did manage to track them down and my suspicions were confirmed. Brian was the neighbourhood know-it-all, your go-to guy for all that went on in the hood. One of the things that probably hurt the most about that incident was that those guys had no idea what they had taken away from me. They couldn't have known that in that laptop I had valuable documentation and how for months I had laboured, writing about the things happening around me.

After that I felt like giving up.

They robbed me, took my laptop, my cell phone and some cash I had in my pocket. What they took wasn't enough because they still had the balls to beat me like a punching bag before they left. Even Floyd Mayweather would have begged for mercy on that one. The only reason why I'm still alive is God's mercy. They broke my heart, but not my spirit and that's the reason why I had enough strength to write it again, starting from page one on a blank A4 exercise book. The words have changed, but the story remains the same. Take whatever you like from me, but you can't take away my experiences. Sometimes I wonder if our government cares about the rate of crime that happens in the inner city or if they have become complacent about what happens to ordinary citizens, as they call us.

Screw it, let's do it: I do a TEDx Talk

Gullan and Gullan are like a family to me. Together with them we didn't just create a website and play our part in Mandela Day; they did more than that for me. I love Gullan and Gullan because they care about what I stand for.

When I received an email invitation to speak at TEDx Johannesburg I didn't know who or what TEDx was but because I'm always chasing knowledge I never feel embarrassed or shy to ask about something that I know nothing about. I knew my friend Colin Browne did a lot of public speaking and that if

TEDx was a real deal he had to know about it so I called him.

Mr Browne said that TEDx is good and I should be happy that they invited me to share my story on the TEDx stage. Two days after I spoke to Mr Browne, I met Dean for lunch at Doppio Zero. He made it sound more exciting. The more he told me about TEDx, the more I got excited about it. I was now confident to tell my friends at Gullan and Gullan about the invitation to give a talk at TEDx. For them it was a big deal and they were happy for me. They told me *Philani, for this one you need to be extra prepared*, and asked me if I had started preparing my talk. I told them I didn't think that it would be necessary because I was too shy to stand in front of so many people.

Desiree Gullan told me not to worry because they would find me a professional to help me develop my confidence. My answer to that was that I don't believe anybody can teach somebody how not to be shy. She told me that it has worked for many people before me and that she hoped it would work for me too. Two days later Kathryn called me and said I had an appointment with Marion Scher, the lady who would coach me so that I could take the stage at TEDx Johannesburg and tell my story to the audience with confidence.

Marion was like an angel who came to my rescue. She made a big difference from our first session. Marion told me that there was nothing wrong with me and that I should remember that nobody is more important than me in this world, no matter how much money or power the next person has. We are all the same in the Creator's eyes. Those words made a huge difference to me and the way I looked at the world; I was used to people looking down on me, I was always worried about being judged.

When people always say mean things about you, you end up not liking them. You think everybody staring at you is thinking of something stupid to say about you. You end up thinking that every group of people looking at you is gossiping or saying something negative about you. That's been my experience since my childhood. I was teased because my eyes are crooked, but my eyes were not my only problem, everything about me was irregular. I have already told you how much of a mission it was for uMa to try to keep me alive.

What I didn't tell you is that because I was a victim of malnutrition, uMa and Mrs Smith had to teach me how to walk because when all my peers could walk I was still crawling. My body was weak, but my two angels didn't want to accept defeat. My mother and Mrs Smith did everything they could to help me live a normal life like every other child. Mrs Smith dug deep into her deeper pockets and made sure uMa had all the financial support we needed and uMa gave me what I can only call unconditional love.

To this day, I don't really know how I managed to survive, but here I am, a living miracle very much alive today. I can walk wherever I want to go, I use the same legs, which once couldn't walk, to run away from Johannesburg's lazy criminals. They don't want to go job hunting because others slave for them; they'll just come and take whatever they want at knife or gun point. Although I see clearly, people who think that they are perfect still make fun of my squint. I have become a man and have developed a thick skin so whatever they say about me doesn't break me anymore. When they laugh at me, I simply smile and walk away.

I never fought with anyone for making stupid remarks about how I look. My mother told me that fighting is a foolish man's hobby. If you smile and walk away, you've got nothing to regret. Now that I'm a grown up, people still have a lot of bull to say about me. One good thing that comes with being an adult is that no matter how many bad things people have to say about you, only a few have the balls to say it straight to your face. Most people just gossip.

I learned a lot from Marion while we were preparing for my TEDx talk. Gullan and Gullan were willing to pay for her time but being the angel that she is Marion trained me free of charge and she gave it her best. Marion transformed me. Before she coached me I always hid behind my shades. I used to wear sunglasses all the time but now I only wear them when I feel like it and not because I'm so shy that I have to, because I was coached by one South Africa's best coaches.

Allow me to tell you why I say she's one of South Africa's best. Marion Scher runs training courses for many of South Africa's top companies on media-related subjects, from writing skills to handling media interviews. In 2005, she was awarded the prestigious Rosalynn Carter award for Mental Health Journalism by The Carter Centre in Atlanta, Georgia, USA. Marion has been a freelance journalist for more than 21 years. I have many more reasons to call her the best but there's a lot to tell about my journey with her and I have got so little time, but I will say this: she made me work really hard preparing my speech, making me say it to her again and again until she was satisfied that I was ready to take the stage.

We had our training sessions in the boardroom of Gullan

and Gullan mostly. They were all very busy so Marion went the extra mile by picking me up from Greenside to do our training at her house. All her efforts paid off because I was able to tell her my story while looking her in the eyes. That was a big challenge for me because I grew up knowing that looking at an adult in the eyes when talking is a sign of being disrespectful.

My culture is in me – I don't want to lose it; in fact, I want to pass it to my kids. But I had to adapt because I would be telling my story to people from different backgrounds. Some of them knew nothing about me, who I was and where I was from or what the correct behaviour is in my culture. Maybe some of them didn't know or care about other people's cultures. To them, it wouldn't make sense that looking at an elder in the eyes is a sign of being disrespectful. Marion had to work extra hard on that one. Finally she won because the more I practised, the more I was able to speak to her and other people without feeling guilty about looking at them in the eyes.

Things were coming together just fine. Though it was hard for me to adapt, I had the best team of friends behind me like Marion, who was a captain, Gullan and Gullan, Gifted Young Leaders, Deborah Strydom, Lisa Skinner, Linda Watson, Dean Lotter, Peter Walters and Colin J Browne. Though Angela Lewis is not in Africa, I could feel the love that she was sending all the way from the United Kingdom. The curator of TEDx Johannesburg, Mr Ithateng Mugoro also helped. That guy's got brains – if I hadn't listened to his advice my talk wouldn't have had as much impact as it did. TEDx Johannesburg was at the Forum in Bryanston on 21 August 2014. I worked closely with Mr Mugoro, sending him my notes, which he read and commented on. We Skyped and we did some media interviews.

I remember an interview at a radio station called Cliff Central. While he was at the studio, I was at Greenside selling books. They gave me a call, though I don't remember what questions they asked or how I replied. I'd like to think that I did better on the next one on SAFM because I was more relaxed. I was still in bed when my phone rang and the producer of the show told me to get ready because they were going to put me on air. I felt more comfortable for that one because I was indoors and not selling books on the noisy streets. But my friend Denzel Taylor, who is head of news at Power FM, still believes that the best ever radio interview I did was with Power FM.

My talk at TEDx almost didn't happen because I almost missed it. A friend who promised to take me there let me down so I was left stranded. Fortunately another friend gave me a ride but dropped me at Sandton, and from there I took a taxi thinking it was going to Bryanston. When I realised I was going in the wrong direction I asked the driver to drop me off and called Kathryn to fetch me and take me to the venue. Being the angel that she is, she dropped everything she was doing and drove straight to where I was stuck and took me to the venue.

The venue was packed, and the speakers' list was also packed. There were 28 speakers including Prof. Justin J Kennedy (neuroscientist, researcher psychologist), Dr Andre Vermeulen (workplace-learning specialist), Ralph Mathekga (political analyst), Marco Cianfanelli (artist), Tony Leon (politician, diplomat), Dr Jeannette McGill (economic geologist, mineral economist), Manda Nkuhlu (social housing investor), Dr Maria Phalime (doctor turned award-winning author), Ingrid

Martens (documentary filmmaker), Dr Jasper Grosskurth (futurist, African markets specialist), Dr Barry Dwolatzky (tech visionary), Dr Michaella Janse van Vuuren (designer, artist, engineer), Marianne Fassler (fashion designer), Dr Musa Mhlanga (molecular biophysicist), Mandla Maseko (the 'afronaut' – he's set to be the first black African in space) and many others.

Some of the things they spoke about I couldn't relate to. But from Ingrid's talk I did pick up a thing or two – her talk about Africa under one roof spoke to me. She was speaking about the Ponte building and the variety of people and about the stereotyping we assume as human beings.

I'd like to believe that as speakers we gave it our best. I'd like to thank the audience for listening attentively. I hope that they learned as much as they were hoping to learn that day. I won't lie – for me it was a good experience. TEDx Johannesburg introduced me to some good new friends and I met wise and interesting people.

After TEDx, it was back to working hard, and that's where Mr Busani Ngcaweni comes in. Busani is my mentor. He is an author, an avid reader, a youth worker and a senior government official. Actually, Mr Ngcaweni made this book possible. When he saw my story on SABC 2's *Morning Live*, Busani made an effort to get in touch with me. He called sis Ayanda, the journalist from SABC who interviewed me, to say he saw my story on the show and he was more than willing to help me write my book and get it published. My sister Ayanda was happy to see that something good had come out of that story we did, and she was very excited when she gave me the news. For me it was a step closer to achieving one of my lifelong dreams, to write a book and get it published.

My liberation diaries

WITHOUT A DOUBT GOD WAS still with me, still loving me and proving that not one of my prayers was ignored. If you have faith, God will amaze you. God has always answered my prayers and I'm sure if I had been praying for money I would be worth millions by now. But I never prayed for money, I prayed for things that make more sense. I remember the last time Busani Ngcaweni and I met; he was launching a good book that he had edited called *Liberation Diaries: Reflections on 20 Years of Democracy*. This guy was brave to edit a book like this, giving a critique of the state of democracy in South Africa since the first democratic elections in 1994. Upon reading it, it struck me that although this guy worked for the Presidency and belonged to the ANC ruling party, he edited a book that had critical things to say about government. After Googling him, I realised that Ngcaweni had established himself as a writer and public intellectual. Here I was thinking these guys in government have hectic lives juggling day jobs and public life.

At a Melville book launch, Ngcaweni was kind enough to give me time on stage so that I could tell the audience about my forthcoming book and myself. He also introduced me to many interesting South Africans including his son Mhlengi Wandile Ngcaweni, who also wrote a chapter in *Liberation Diaries*; and Mr Eric Myeni, who is also an author of books. Captured by my story, Eric Myeni kindly gave me 10 copies of his book, *A Letter from Paris* and complemented Ngcaweni for sharing his time and platform with me.

That afternoon I also met a lovely lady called Malaika wa Azania, who was launching her book entitled *Memoirs of a Born Free,* and many other people who are passionate about books. That's not all that Busani did for me – he went the extra mile to help my good friend Leizl Eykelhof, who is as passionate about getting kids reading as I am.

Leizl's dream is to create a children's magazine to help make kids fall in love with reading at a young age. I liked her idea because I had always wanted to run a children's writing competition where kids write their stories and we choose the ten best stories to edit and make into a nice kiddies' book. If the magazine became a reality many kids would be challenged to write their own stories and have fun. What they'll be unaware of is that they will also be learning while having fun. When learning is fun kids will look forward to the next lesson. Leizl works hard to get people to sponsor our kids' magazine. We often meet once if not twice a week to discuss and meet potential sponsors who can help with funding. Often nothing comes of it because people and companies are more worried about making more money instead of how they can make their extra money useful to make this country a better place.

It's hard to see a good thing even if it's right in front of you. Liezl and I both want this magazine to happen and it breaks our hearts after all the effort and the love we've been giving to this baby, that not one organisation or person with enough financial power believes in us. R500 000 would enable us to give a thousand kids something new to read every month for the whole year and the magazine will be available free. Both Leizl and myself are dedicated to getting kids reading. We won't make a cent out of this and just want children to be excited to read a magazine and learn from it and share their excitement and love for reading and look forward to the next issue. Our payment will be the smiles on their faces and the knowledge that we played our part. Is that too much to ask for? We are not out to enrich ourselves but to enrich the minds of our future leaders. If we want to live in a better South Africa, we should open up our hearts and start uplifting others.

All these encounters liberated me from the anxiety of wondering whether or not my book will ever be published. In a sense, this diary of encounters liberated me.

For South Africa to improve we need more people like Peter

Walters, Busani Ngcaweni, Dean Lotter, Leizl Eykelhof, DJ Sbu, Mike and Desiree Gullan, Lisa Skinner, Deborah Strydom, Cynthia Robson and many other people who have helped me to help my kids. Please don't say, *He is only telling us about his friends which we know nothing about and don't care about.* If you could be so kind as to take the old books you no longer need, or buy stationery or a pair of school shoes for one needy kid out there, your name could make it to that list. To some people, less is more – they didn't have to donate hundreds of thousands to make a difference. Do you think the kid who you bought their first pair of school shoes for will forget who you are?

Stop being greedy! When was the last time you gave to the needy? I might not have millions in my bank account but if you put a millionaire and Philani Dladla in the middle of Joburg city central and asked the kids who they'd like to spend a week with or who they'd want to be like when they grow up chances are that the kids will choose me. Kids don't care about how much money or flashy things you have; they only care about how much you care about them. Kids don't care about what you can give them in the future; they care about what you gave them in the past. They don't care about what you can do for them, they care about what you already did for them. Everything you see out there started as a dream, so dream a better dream and work hard to make it a reality. Have dreams that will improve other people's lives. Stop dreaming about money – too much money is not enough money, if you love money, you will be chasing paper until the day you die.

I like how simple and good our education system was when

I was in primary school. When I was in Standard 3, my class teacher Mr Ngubane made everything easy to understand for us learners. When he defined the word *history*, he told us that history tells us about people, history tells us what people did at different times and in different places. You don't need to be a politician or a war hero to make history. Many years from today, when people tell people about you, where you lived and what you did, history will be remembering you. Just like some people started successful businesses with less than R10, you can improve many people's lives with what you have today. Please start with what you have today because if you wait until you have enough money, I'm afraid you're going to have to wait forever.

I always hear people say *I have got a lot of money* but I have never heard anyone say, *I have enough money*. I often hear people talking about their success stories, but I never hear people say, *I always wanted to be successful but first I had to wait to have enough money to make me the success story that I am today*. Successful people made the most of what they had in order to create what they have today. DJ Sbu likes saying *procrastination will slaughter your dreams*. If you believe that you can do it, don't let anybody tell you that you're not good enough. I'm giving you my stamp of approval. *Yes you can do it!* History has shown us over and over that ordinary people are capable of achieving greatness.

You can decide to step out of the ordinary right now. Go and make things happen for a struggling child who needs financial assistance so she focuses on her studies without worrying. My dear reader, complaining won't make things better, complaining won't solve problems.

Let's be a generation of Doers! Let us make things happen for our families, our communities, our country, this beautiful African continent and the whole world. Complaining is just a waste of our precious time. When you see something that makes you unhappy about living in your country, before you blame the government, first ask yourself what you as an individual can do to change it. Ask what needs to be done. How? Is there anything you can do to make things better? You should always find a solution to a problem instead of making silly comments and pointing fingers. How can you expect government to change something that you don't know how you would change if you were in government?

Hope is good. I know how dangerous being hopeless is: hopelessness is a poison that kills young, beautiful, talented South Africans every day. Young brothers do crime and don't care if they get killed or arrested because they don't have any hope left. There is no light at the end of the tunnel for them because they believe that they were born to suffer.

A lot of creative, talented brothers are crammed into prisons around South Africa – Durban Westville, Sun City, to the C-max prison in Pretoria. Some are lying six feet under because they lost hope and resorted to desperate measures. Many of my beautiful sisters can be found in all corners of our big cities and small towns selling sex. See how dangerous hopelessness can be? I mean how can you earn a living out of sleeping with different men every day? Prostitution is a quick way of making money and to the grave for my sisters because many are HIV positive. Sex with a different man every hour of every day can only lead to disaster for that person. Our sisters are brave and being brave is good but our sisters are stupidly brave. They sleep with men whether he uses protection or not. It's okay as long as he has money. If a man has a car, girls treat him like a king; they even kiss his behind.

The reality is that HIV/AIDS doesn't care how fancy your car is, or how much money you have in the bank. At the end of the day, these brave sisters get all the money they want but also the bonus they didn't need – HIV, or even worse, AIDS. Precious lives get wasted because of desperation. That's why I say hopelessness is dangerous.

I don't want to see any of the kids in my book club feeling hopeless. I want them to go to school and look forward to a better future. I want them to know that there are people out there who believe in them. If prisoners can get out of jail after so many years and govern a country, surely a kid who is growing up under extreme poverty in downtown Joburg can grow up to be a successful entrepreneur, astronaut, doctor or influential politician? They can be all that and more if only people believed in and invested in them. Nelson Mandela cared about our future leaders. When the first group of kids from my club graduate from college my greatest wish is that he will look down and smile.

Just like I refused to let my life be destroyed by drugs, I will also refuse to let being poor prevent me from living my dream. I often see families dining together at fancy restaurants and I promise myself that someday my kids will have the financial power from their education to take their families to those same fancy restaurants. I live in a world where everything is possible.

I love everything inspirational – that's why I read those sorts of books. I admire the courage of entrepreneurs like Doctor Richard Maponya, Sir Richard Branson, and guys like Jack Walsh, Alan Knott-Craig and the many others who have built empires from the ground up and led big companies for many years, growing them from strength to strength. I like peace, I like people who dream big, I like growth, I like nature, I like diversity, and most of all I like Africa. I'm proud to be a South African and I don't want to even begin to imagine living in a South Africa where Nelson Mandela never existed. He made South Africa the land of opportunities it is today. Every time I read about other African countries in newspapers, all I see is sadness written on innocent people's faces.

Many Africans don't know the difference between a white man and a coloured man – for them they're both the same. Some think all white men are English because they never grew up in a Rainbow Nation like ours. Their leaders were filled with hatred and anger. They never thought about the end results of their decisions and now thousands, if not millions, of innocent people are suffering today. They only took time to plan revenge. There are some African countries who've been at war from the day I was born on 27 February in 1989. I bet those countries wish they'd their own icon like Nelson Mandela whose name history will remember for hundreds of years to come.

I can't just hate somebody because that somebody is from a different race, tribe or religion. I read the newspapers and see sad stories about Muslims killing Christians. Millions of Christian men, women and children have been bombed and shot just because of their religion. I have got only one God and he is the almighty Creator. If I have to be judged for my religion I would die standing up for what I believe in. I have never killed or hated any man, woman or a child because they belong to a different religion than mine and I'm going to keep it that way.

My Bible doesn't teach me to hate, it teaches me to love because God is love. I love life, I love seeing people happy, I like seeing people making their dreams becoming a reality, not like those losers who keep complaining about how unfair life is. I like doers who make things happen no matter how hard life is. I like being around people whose dreams sometimes frighten them because they are bigger than your average dreams.

I don't like being around the complainers who always make excuses for themselves and blame others for their misfortunes and failures. They see others making moves and working hard but choose to waste their time complaining about how hard and unfair life is. They forget that nobody has it easy and are always unhappy, envious under-achievers.

In townships you find bitter, lazy young people sitting indoors for the whole day eating, smoking and sleeping, just wasting food and stressing poor parents. If you suggest job hunting or starting a small business they say they won't start a small business slaving for peanuts but are waiting for their turn to win the lottery. They gamble for years without any luck and never read the fine print that says *winners know when to stop*. Some can't read and those that can don't know what it means. I was reading a local book entitled *African Cook Boy* the other day and learned that real luck is what you make yourself by using your hands and your head.

———•✦•———

I believe, the reason why our streets and our cities are filled with street kids is because kids' minds are dirty. A kid can tell you that they have got rights but a kid won't tell you that they have got responsibilities. Teen pregnancy is so high because fathers warn their daughters about the kind of boys they go out with, only to have their daughters act 'smart'. When parents try to show teenage boys the right way to go in life, boys start complaining that parents want to control them or say they hate or abuse them. Then they leave home and decide to live on the streets and people call them homeless.

If you take the train off the track it is free, but where does it go? It's derailed. If everybody was free to take or do whatever they want, anywhere, anytime, would you call that freedom or chaos? Child abuse is wrong and should never happen, but the youth should know the difference between discipline and abuse. You can't just leave a comfortable home and go live on the streets and say your parents are abusing you because you want to make your own stupid rules. Kids need to know that parents want what's best for them. As soon as they learn that, there will be fewer homeless people on the streets.

Drugs led me to good people. I'm not saying you should try them because I know they'll kill you, turn you into a hobo or destroy your dreams. My life has been an adventure, but if you think drugs are going to make yours one too you're mistaken. You'll get lost in your own adventure and drugs will slaughter your dreams. What some might have survived for years can kill you on your first day for we aren't all the same. Others have tried but they didn't make it, and are resting six feet under. Some lucky ones swallowed their empty pride and went back to wherever they came from to make peace with the people they wronged or the parents they ran away from. Those who sleep on the pavement don't often get sick, because there's no space for sissy guys or girls out there and they have already developed thick skins, their bodies adapted a long time ago.

I can tell you one thing, everybody belongs somewhere. Everybody has a family despite what I have told you about my father's cruel family and how they treated uMa and me. Especially for us black South Africans, both your mother and father can die and you might be left alone, but if you respect people and respect yourself you will always have a family, because the spirit of *ubuntu* never dies. Your neighbours, uncles, aunts and your grandparents can always give you a place to call home and people to call family. This is why our parents teach us to have respect. They tell us that any lady of your mum's age is your mother and every man of your father's age is your father.

———

My story does not end here. This is just the beginning. The Pavement Bookworm Foundation is now up and running, and people are donating books, dictionaries and other learner support material. I am invited to speak at important gatherings. My network of book clubs is expanding daily: all the hallmarks of progress and success.

I have a plan to manufacture Pavement Bookworm bookmarks that will be available from my website, my mobile bookshop and any other shop that cares about making a difference. My bookmarks will sell for R20 each and every bookmark sold will go toward supporting children. My aim is to make school exciting for my kids – I want them to look forward to going to school every day when the sun rises. I believe in myself and in the book readers who buy books from me. I know we will make this work.

I have a great plan to make my goals a reality. My plan is to set up a non-profit to raise funds to pay for the kids in my readers' club to go to college after Grade 12. As long as I'm alive, I want to give kids reasons to look forward to going to school every day and to do well in their studies. A lot of kids don't care about going to school. If you ask them why they don't like school, they tell you that their sisters and brothers passed Grade 12 but are still not working and so for them going to school is just a waste of time. They didn't even go to college. I want to change that. I want kids to do well at school because they hope to do well enough to go to university or college when they finish.

Some day soon, I will tell you all about it. One thing is for sure: I ain't gonna die yet and drugs will never win against me. No circumstance, as traumatic as it can be, will break me: I am the Pavement Bookworm after all!

Acknowledgements

THERE ARE JUST TOO MANY PEOPLE to thank for the life and opportunities I have had in my nearly three decades in this world. If I listed all those who have touched my life, the ink would run dry before I could finish. This chronicle mentions many people who contributed to the making of Philani Dladla, the Pavement Bookworm.

For the purposes of this book project, I wish to thank the following people: Busani Ngcaweni for taking the challenge of editing and producing this book when it all seemed a distant dream that one day I will have my name on the cover of a book. Thabiso Mahlape, thank you my sister for believing in me and associating your new publishing imprint, BlackBird Books, with this book. Hope we will publish and work together more!

Thank you Adelaide Steedly, 'my mother from America', for opening your home to me and investing many hours reading through and commenting on the manuscript. My brother's keeper Leizel Mattison-Eykelhof, Dudu Mazibuko-Nchoba and Nozipho Mbanjwa, your support is much appreciated.

Desiree, Kathryn and the whole Gullan and Gullan family, much is said about you in this book. For now I say, salute!

DJ Sbu Leope, I run out of words of gratitude when I think of your contribution in my life. I dare say, I am alive today because of you.

Truth be told, I would be an unknown entity today had it not been for the film-maker who made a YouTube feature about me that went viral. Tebogo Malope, *imisebenzi yakho iyabonakala!*

My brother and role model, Phillip Ramphisa. Thank you for being there for me when most people turned a blind eye on me. Remember the worst days, when I was in hospital and your car got stolen while you were visiting me. You kept me going when I was stuck back home in KZN. Even when most people were too busy for me, you never were.

Peter Walters, my heavenly sent brother. Honestly I am out of words, P. Thank you for being a part of this adventure, tears are running down my face as I write this. Even though you are younger than me, you have been like a big brother to me since the day we met. I thank God for introducing me to you, bro.

You have saved my life in many ways. Much love, I wish you and Sarah a happy and healthy marriage and many kids.

Dean Lotter, I don't even want to imagine where I would be without you. You have made a big impact in my life and I know how much you want to see me do well in life. Thank you for the lessons, the support, for listening and for all the wisdom you shared with me. You are a rock star.

To the whole BBC (Bryanston Bible Church) community, thank you for praying for me when I was going through some of the worst days of my life. Unfortunately Pastor Roisleg, I don't have R1.9 million to buy you a car.

Thabiso Ndimbane and Brian at Park Court, thank you for your loyalty and your ongoing support; I'm proud to call you guys my brothers. Mcendisi, Qubu and Motheo, we are gifted young leaders, keep up the good work. May we continue changing young people's lives and I know that should I not be there, you will represent me well.

Thank you to every single one from Wits Univeristy who supported and encouraged my business. I would not be here, were it not for you.

To friends who buy books from me in Greenside and those who always make time to meet up with me at Doppio Zero, I love and value you all.

Alison Dupen and Fiona Tipping, I have nothing but love and respect for you my lovely friends.

Dr Edith Phaswana, thank you for driving all around Gauteng collecting book donations from people's houses and letting me use your garage as a storage space. You and your daughter remain in my heart always.

Katie Engelbrecht, I have learnt so much from you in a short span of time. I enjoy working with you. I especially love how real you are. I hope to do this with you for many more years, my sister.